WORLD

OF

GIVING

Jeffrey Inaba and C-Lab

Columbia University GSAPP
New Museum
Lars Müller Publishers

Authors
Jeffrey Inaba
Katharine Meagher

Editor
Jason Zuzga

Designers
Daniella Spinat
Daniel Koppich

Collaborators
Kumar Atre, Talene Montgomery, Julianne Gola,
Hilla Rudanko, Jeremy Alain Siegel, Day Jimenez,
Liz Stetson, Cody Campanie, Anabelle Pang,
Dana Karwas, Winnie Lam, Shumi Bose, April Lee,
Lukas Pauer, Aurelien Gillier, Evan Litvin,
Simon Battisti, Mariela Alvarez, Matthew Clarke,
Andrew Shimomura, Jesse Seegers,
Elizabeth Knotts

Publisher
Lars Müller Publishers, Baden, Switzerland
www.lars-muller-publishers.com

Production
Marion Plassmann

Printer/Binder
Freiburger Graphische Betriebe, Germany

Givers
C-Lab would like to acknowledge the following
friends for their support and guidance throughout
the development this book: Mark Wigley, Lisa
Phillips, Richard Flood, Lars Müller, Karen Wong,
Katharina Kulke, David Hinkle, Janet Reyes,
Jessica Braun, Leslie Bailey, Benedict Clouette,
Glen Cummings, Jason Long, Gavin Browning,
Lewis Lapham, Jiang Jun, Reinhold Martin,
Michael Rock, Geoff Manaugh, Joseph Grima,
Arianna Huffington, Chris Anderson, Rene Daalder,
David Benjamin, Janette Kim, Kazys Varnelis.

Partners
Columbia University Graduate School
of Architecture Planning and Preservation
New Museum

ISBN 978-3-03778-181-4

Love you, Lea! I hope this may keep you in good company on your upcoming adventure!

Contents

1
Given

In 1847, during the Great Irish Famine (1845–1849), a group of Choctaw American Indians collect 710 USD and give it to starving Irish men, women and children. Adjusted for inflation this amounts to 14,178.21 USD, but due to the tremendous strife of the Choctaw people at that time, the gift has been likened to a million dollars. Just sixteen years before, the Choctaw people had experienced the Trail of Tears, the forced barefoot march from their homelands to "Indian Territory," during which many died of diseases and starvation.[1]

In Kansas City, Missouri, Claudine Jackson spends two years on a national kidney waiting list. Her next-door neighbor, Jo Ann Walz, gives Jackson car rides to dialysis treatment, doctor's appointments and the grocery store. To move Jackson off the waiting list, Walz also gives her kidney to Jackson.[2]

Cochise, a vessel competing in a trans-Atlantic sailing rally, loses its mast 866 miles from shore. The skipper of a competing vessel, the *Belle*, hears the call for help on a VHS frequency, tacks to the other boat and transfers 200 liters of fuel to the *Cochise* mid-sea, via the *Belle's* dinghy.[3]

During the Great European Famine (1315–1317), a period of hunger and disease caused by crop-failure, the elderly refuse food, giving away their shares with the hope that younger generations might survive.[4]

Escaped slave Harriet Tubman returns to give other slaves freedom by taking them north along the Underground Railroad. She makes nineteen trips back to the South and "conducts" 300 slaves to freedom, never losing a single person. By 1856, 40,000 USD is offered for her capture.[5]

In 1948, Sister Teresa leaves her convent in Ireland to give her life to the poor, sick and dying of Calcutta, India. Having no money, expertise or power to give, she offers intelligence and persistence. She converts an abandoned Hindu temple into the Kalighat Home for the Dying, a free hospice that gives poor people a place to die with dignity.[6]

Sweden is the only western country that gives entry to any Iraqi who can prove having fled central or southern Iraq. The Swedish Migration Board states that this policy is not conditional, even considering the refugee's political involvement or circumstances of arrival in Sweden, which often involves forged passports and extensive smuggler's networks.[7]

In the mountainous terrain of Ladakh in northern India, Tibetan Buddhist families give in sacrifice their most precious possession—a white yak. Upon a mountain and under the eye of the priest, the yak is not slain, but set free into the wilderness.[8]

Margaret Delfino, ninety-year-old great-grandmother, began giving blood in 1954. She donated regularly until 2001, when she was diagnosed with ovarian cancer. After five years of treatment, her doctors declare her cancer-free, and she resumes giving. Over the course of her life, she has donated more than twenty-five gallons of blood.[9]

New York Times reports on December 8, 1931 that the US people had given to their Community Chests 14.9 percent more than in 1930. It was noted that the economic strife of the Great Depression coincided with a rapid growth in individual giving, especially within one's own community.[10]

Early Jewish synagogues designated spaces for the kindly deposit and distribution of alms. Donors give anonymous gifts in one room of the temple. Beneficiaries collect the offerings in a second room, unseen by contributors, and thus remain immune from any shame in the transaction.[11]

On January 13, 1982, an Air Florida Boeing 727 plunges into Washington, D.C.'s freezing Potomac River. Arland Williams survives the crash and gives rescue lifelines to others rather than take one for himself. Lenny Skutnik watches the unfolding tragedy from a bridge, then jumps into the water and swims to a passenger unable to keep a grip on a lifeline. Williams is the only plane passenger to die from drowning. The Reagan administration gives Skutnik and Williams the Coast Guard Gold Lifesaving Medal. The bridge is renamed the Arland D. Williams Jr. Memorial Bridge.[12]

During the Potlatch ceremonies practiced by indigenous peoples of northwest America, the family leader hosts guests—friends and neighbors—among whom property is distributed as gifts: material wealth like foods and goods or non-material things like songs and dances. The status of a given family is determined not by who possesses the most resources, but by who gives the most.[13]

Clandestine knowledge of procedures to prepare herbs to induce abortion is given by women from the West Indies to women in Europe during the 1600s.[14]

The Metropolitan Transit Authority of New York City imposes fines between twenty-five and fifty USD to motivate passengers to give their seats on subways and buses to the elderly and disabled. A 2009 poster campaign reminds riders that "not all disabilities are visible," in an effort to reintroduce the courteous practice.[15]

In 1963, Dutch brewer Alfred Heineken grows concerned both about beaches littered with bottles and with the Third World's lack of affordable building material. He develops the Heineken WOBO (world bottle) as a gift to answer both concerns. The "brick that holds beer" is stackable and can thus provide a material for homes. Heineken is ready to modify his production methods for the sake of the poor, but his brewery does not support the idea.[16]

Steel baron Andrew Carnegie (1835–1919) creates a model he calls Scientific Philanthropy. He funds more than 2,500 free libraries around the world, the first to feature open stacks for browsing. He considers it shameful to die wealthy, without having distributed one's possessions fairly.[17]

A whole congregation of US Catholic nuns give their brains to Alzheimer research in 1986. The congregation of School Sisters of Notre Dame Nuns volunteer as a research group for the University of Missouri: all the nuns over seventy-five years of age are dedicated to taking part and gifting their brains upon death. The similarity of their adult lives functions as an effective experimental control.[18]

Samoan tribes are given blue bead necklaces from the first Dutch expeditions in the seventeenth century. Subsequently, these necklaces can be used to save one's life after a battle when given by a prisoner to the victors. This tradition is called *togiola* or "life-giving."[19]

In October 2008, British rock band Radiohead releases their album *In Rainbows*—their first ever self-release—as a gift. In a move that surprises record companies and industry insiders alike, all ten tracks are downloadable for free. The altruism of the offer catches Radiohead's skeptical fan base off-guard— despite the music being completely free, almost twice as many copies are downloaded from pirated sources as from the band's official website.[20]

In ancient Greek cities, private patrons fund theatrical festivals by commissioning works from playwrights and furnishing teams of actors. Audiences judge each play, and the patrons of the winning production erect beautiful monuments at their own cost commemorating themselves as philanthropists. These public monuments shape the urban environment and allow sculptors to experiment and develop the plastic arts and architecture.[21]

In November 2007, New Jersey dentist Howard Lassin joins Operation Smile in Linyi, China, assisting plastic surgeons who operate on children and young adults with cleft palates and other facial deformities. Lassin notes that while abroad he was attempting to fulfill the Jewish tenet of *tikkun olam*, or, "the repairing of the world."[22]

K Foundation funds—earned by the successful 1990s pop group The KLF—were originally intended as grants for struggling artists. Instead, the duo comprising the Foundation decides to make something, rather than fund something, with the money. *K Foundation Burn a Million Quid* takes place on August 23, 1994 when the K Foundation gives one million pounds sterling in cash, the bulk of the Foundation's funds, to be burnt on the Scottish island of Jura.[23]

Sri Lankan Prime Minister, Laxman Kadirgamar, accepts a box of teddy bears after the Indian Ocean tsunami in 2004 as a gift for children affected by the disaster. He states that such donations are useless.[24]

Gilded Age philanthropist John D. Rockefeller (1839–1937) has a habit of throwing dimes to children as he walks by. During the Depression in the 1920s, he continues the habit, but switches to nickels.[25]

After a fruitless ten-year siege of Troy, the Greeks build a huge figure of a horse in which hide a select force of soldiers. The Greeks place it at the city gates and pretend to sail away, while the Trojans pull the gift into their city as a victory trophy. During the night, the Greek force creeps out and opens the gates for their advancing army. Although ignored, the priest Laocoön had guessed the plot and given the Trojans a warning: "Do not trust Greeks bearing gifts!"[26]

In May 2009, the US Federal Government gives 34.5 million Americans assistance to buy food. The Supplemental Nutrition Assistance Program (SNAP) is one of the country's oldest social welfare projects and accounts for thirteen percent of all domestic aid.[27] The original beneficiary of the food stamp program was twofold—poor urban families and rural farmers with fiscally dangerous surpluses of grain.[28]

Robert Mugabe is a hero in the West during the 1980s, known for his outspoken opposition to apartheid. As a result of his admirable contributions to the struggle for human rights, many US universities give him their most esteemed gift—the honorary doctorate. Later the givers will renounce these gifts after they learn of atrocities attributed to Mugabe.[29]

Euthanasia in Oregon, Washington, Holland and Belgium is now is typically carried out by giving a series of injections nearly identical to those used in US prisons.[30]

In 2001, so many westerners give clothes to the Salvation Army that the charity lacks the labor to unpack many of the donations. Instead, they sell the clothes, strapped and packed in bales like hay, to companies for commercial for-profit export to Third World countries.[31]

Tata Group is the largest private corporation in India and also an enormous corporate philanthropic entity. The company gives about thirty percent of its profits after tax to social development in India, financing research, education and culture, making it one of the government's most important partners.[32]

Christopher Columbus gives red caps, glass beads and other objects to the Indians he encounters during his first expeditions on the American continent. He wins their trust and receives other gifts in exchange: a trade relationship is established.[33]

Despite being only in theaters, a family friend contacts Pixar Studios to arrange a DVD copy of its film *Up!* for Colby Curtin, a 10 year old stricken with vascular cancer. An employee brings the film to the Curtins' house along with stuffed animals of the films characters. Colby dies later that night.[34]

The 1953 Iranian coup d'état, funded by the US and British governments, deposes the democratically elected Prime Minister Mosaddeq. Mosaddeq had angered Britain in 1951 by nationalizing Iran's oil industry, previously ruled by the British. In 1952, British and US spy agencies commence Operation Ajax to replace the government with an all-powerful monarch. In April 1953, the CIA approves one million USD to be used "in any way that would bring about the fall of Mosaddeq." The new Iranian government signed the Consortium Agreement with the US and UK, giving US and UK oil companies an even split of eighty percent of Iranian oil profits.[35]

In 2001, Russian oligarch Roman Abramovich is elected governor of the impoverished region Chukotka in the Russian far east. During his seven-year governorship he gives over 1.3 billion USD of his own money to build schools, hospitals and public welfare in the region, which now has one of the highest birth rates in Russia. In 2005, he resigns, as the governorship has become too expensive.[36]

Gifts Are:

Time	Personal info
Money	Body Organs
Blood	Encouragement
Petrol	Appeasement
Directions	Illness
Labor	Hugs
Rights	Witness
Surplus	Cures
Water	First Aid
Shelter	Power Generators
Filtration	Blankets
Emergency kits	Apprenticeship
Land	Water purification
Livestock	Machetes
Lessons	AK-47s
Lifts	Pesticides
Health	Hiding places
Rice	Identity
Praise	Parkas
Promise	GMOs
Advice	Matches
Prayer	Shoes
CPR	Electricity
Contraband	Translation
Assistance	Seeds
Cooking oil	Forgiveness
Transportation	
Tips	

Givers Are:

Sympathizers
Empathizers
Statesmen
Boards
Bleeding hearts
The bored
Optimists
Orphans
Debtors
The put upon
The guilty
Sociopaths
The shamed
Overachievers
Résumé neurotics
Opportunists
The pious
Believers
Deniers
Investors
The lucky
Empire builders
Conservatives
The thoughtful
Self-aggrandizers
Communitarians
Elitists
Egoists

Egalitarians
Victims
The down and out
Survivors
The unlucky
The exploited
The infirm
Siblings
The tired
The hungry
Newborns
Refugees
Taxpayers
Romantics
The doe-eyed
Friends
Neighbors
The deceased
Acquaintances
Strangers
Good daughters
Good sons
Poor huddled
masses

Glossary

Aid
A gift that adds to the existing capacities of a recipient.

Beneficiary
The party that receives a gift, as well as the attention and goodwill of the giving organization.

Bequest
An amount given, or set aside to be given, upon death.

Charity
A nonprofit organization that engages in awareness raising, collection, and some form of distribution.

Development Aid
Gifts that are intended to stimulate economic growth, effectively stabilizing the recipient and diminishing emergent need.

Donation
Something given in support of a cause that one feels is worthy to help an organization's efforts, if not also intended to be passed intact to a recipient.

Donor
One who gives a gift to address a greater need that has been identified and expressed by others or oneself.

Foundation
Either a nonprofit or a charitable trust, formalized by tax law, existing to make grants to unaffiliated institutions and organizations.

Fundraising
Soliciting and gathering gifts to support any particular aim, although most often used in the context of nonprofit work.

Gift
Something that is voluntarily transferred from one entity to another to intentionally produce an effect for both the giver and the recipient.

Giver
One who voluntarily gives a gift to another entity.

Giving
The act of voluntarily transferring something from one entity to another on the basis of either a perceived or articulated need or want.

Mega-giver

A giver who gives in excess of one million USD. A mega-giver typically gives monetarily.

NGO

A voluntary organization not necessarily recognized by local government, organized around a particular, unmet civil need.

Nonprofit

An organization, legally recognized as tax exempt, devoted to the pursuit of a benefit other than that of profit, such as pleasure, education, religious or communal good.

Philanthropist

One who gives deliberately, to support a common good with which they may be personally identified. This title is usually conferred on those who give larger amounts of money.

Philanthropy

The voluntary promotion of human development.

Poverty

The poverty line is established as the minimum daily monetary equivalent for a sufficient standard of living in any given country. The international poverty line is approximately one USD a day.

Private Foundation
A nonprofit or charitable trust, funded by one individual, family or corporate entity that administers grants to unaffiliated entities (organizations or individuals) to carry out work in various sectors such as science, the arts, education or religion.

Public Foundation
A nonprofit or charitable trust, funded by multiple entities—such as government agencies, individual and private foundations—who must be keep diverse in order for the foundation to retain its public status. Grants are administered to unaffiliated entities (organizations or individuals) to carry out work in various sectors such as science, the arts, education or religion.

Recipient
An entity that is either a final and ultimate target of assistance or gifts, or a secondary collection and distribution agency that will then pass assistance or gifts to a final recipient.

Taker
One who receives gifts, either as an end-user or as a middle agent.

Volunteer
An individual who engages in an activity without being monetarily compensated.

Give and Take

In any act of giving, while value and capacity are transferring from one party to another, information flows back and forth in a give and take exchange.

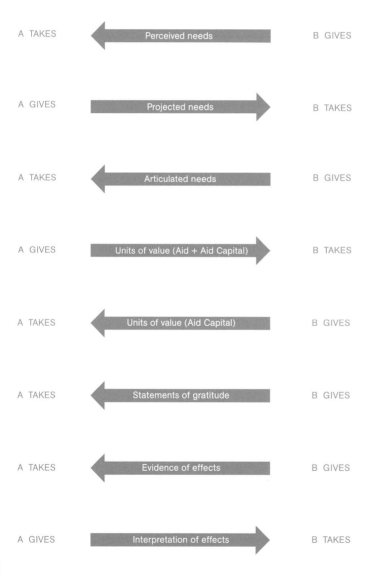

A TAKES	← Perceived needs	B GIVES
A GIVES	Projected needs →	B TAKES
A TAKES	← Articulated needs	B GIVES
A GIVES	Units of value (Aid + Aid Capital) →	B TAKES
A TAKES	← Units of value (Aid Capital)	B GIVES
A TAKES	← Statements of gratitude	B GIVES
A TAKES	← Evidence of effects	B GIVES
A GIVES	Interpretation of effects →	B TAKES

2
Motives

Giving
Jeffrey Inaba

Giving permeates human activity. It is present always and everywhere. All around there are acts of giving, some unintended, others premeditated. Some involve gifts to oneself and some to other people. Without giving there would be no communication. Nothing would be extended and nothing would be received. In its absence, nothing can survive. Giving is essential to our existence; yet, it is literally taken for granted. Its benign nature belies its omnipresence. It is even said that it is most virtuous when it goes unnoticed. It is embedded in so much of what we do, that if one were to stop and think about it, it would be difficult to discern when an action is not giving. While it is so ubiquitous that it goes unseen, on a social level it is easily triggered and multiplies. Little is required for it to take hold, build momentum and spread.

Giving is any act that improves the capacity of another person. A gift can be as little as a nod of encouragement, or as great as taking a bullet for a friend. Often giving assumes the form of money or time for the purposes of supporting a cause or organization, such as a cultural institution, social services program or humanitarian campaign. There are varying channels to send gifts to recipients including private philanthropies, governmental agencies, development banks and NGOs that operate locally, nationally and globally.

Everyone is a giver. Every person gives to themselves; many also give to others. When a recipient acknowledges a gift, the recipient becomes a giver by sending information back in return. Such information can range from an expression of acknowledgement to data about the health of a particular population. Even silence is a form of feedback. Receivers are givers too.

The motives behind giving are never singular, but further, can be comprised of an array of contrary vectors. Giving may be an altruistic gesture of helping another person without consciously expecting something concrete in return. On another level it may be prompted by self-interest, where help is extended to others in order to receive a benefit for oneself. But what is considered a benefit is as complex as each person. Giving may be motivated by a desire to simply receive the warm glow that results from acting generously. Or, one might believe that the greatest gift to oneself is to sacrifice one's life for an important social cause. We suggest that to undermine acts of giving with accusations of self-interest is overly simplistic. The potential positive feedback that flows to the giver is just as integral a part of the dynamic of giving as the positive benefit that flows to the receiver.

Giving can be overshadowed by money. When it is granted public attention, the focus can be on the gift's monetary value as an index of the giver's affluence. The gesture can also appear to be less than altruistic and therefore dismissed as an act of self-advancement— neglecting the gift's actual impact. Or it could be an act that requires relatively little sacrifice on the giver's part, such as lending one's name to a worthy cause. In these instances, the aura of individual success may divert attention from the actual need that called the gift into being or action. Though a gift's economic magnitude can be quite significant, it is only one aspect of the influence aid exerts. Building new associations and cycles of giving is the goal of this book.

Aid Capital is our term for the power of giving. It is the sum of other resources like economic capital (money), political capital (governmental and institutional sway) and human capital (people's time and energy) composed together with the specific desire to increase the capacity of others. Similar to these forms of capital, Aid Capital is accumulated and spent; however, the intention is not to create an advantageous imbalance for one side or the other. Since its purpose is to improve the capacity of others, in order for it to have value, Aid Capital must be transferred from a spender to a receiver. But when it is spent, it does not result in an accumulation of capital by the receiver and in a loss for the giver. Rather, it accumulates as an asset for both.

Aid Capital is plentiful. It is precious but not in scarce supply. Unlike a finite resource within a closed system, there is virtually no limit to its accumulation. In addition to financial and political resources, Aid Capital includes the sum of the willingness of individuals to offer their time. Relatively speaking, such willingness to volunteer is an abundant, renewable and increasable resource. People are inclined to expend their energy if it is clear that it is going toward a purpose they believe in and that no one profits from the value of their generosity.

When Aid Capital is spent, the giver provides the receiver with both aid and Aid Capital. Aid in the form of money, expert knowledge, food or supplies, for example, is delivered to address the recipient's needs. As a result of the transfer, the recipient also gains Aid Capital in the capacity to share and give.

As feedback from the exchange, Aid Capital also flows to the giver. Most often this is by way of better knowledge of how to provide aid, an expanded political network or an elevation in reputation. The Aid Capital returned to the giver increases the giver's ability to acquire more of the limited raw materials (money, intelligence, etc.) for future aid. In addition, this also helps to produce the relatively abundant asset of volunteers' time and energy. New Aid Capital, in the form of a greater number of committed volunteers, is brought into the system, which in turn fuels the opportunity to seek resources like financing and materials, in effect expanding the capital of the system as a whole. In other words, ingredients such as human will—which are unbounded by the material limitations of other resources—contribute greatly to the sum of all assets, including those that are in scarce supply. And because aid flows in two directions, both from and to each giver, there is no terminal recipient; aid is given and taken without end points. Giving is continuous. The net supply grows and the system itself expands.

While it is somewhat possible to recognize, gauge and accept the varying degree of self-interest that motivates giving on an interpersonal level, it is difficult to do so at an institutional scale. When there are more parties (all of whom have different motives), as well as many more channels through which assistance passes, it's not easy to know for sure that one's gift is going toward a desired cause.

A common criticism is that institutional giving is ineffective. There is frequent mention of bureaucratic inefficiency, sub-standard levels of performance when compared to commercial ventures, redundancy of agencies working toward similar ends, exploitation of goodwill and simply, being slow. The examples are so widespread that some believe giving's problem is not a dearth of money, but rather the mismanagement of aid. In certain contexts it is argued to be so broken that it would be best to dissolve large-scale aid altogether. Such a drastic measure is an overreaction. The increase in recent levels of aid would suggest that giving will continue to resist the barriers that jeopardize its delivery, just as it is certain that the obstacles themselves will multiply. While clearly important to address, these challenges will not go away, as they are largely the result of the particular dynamic of exchange—one of give and take.

Large-scale aid undergoes many transformations, or phase changes, between the giver and receiver. In the most basic circumstances, it changes from a promise, to a transfer of funds in one currency, to the holding and verification of the funds, to a distribution of funds in another currency, to the conversion of funds into procured raw materials and resources, to the integration and realization of those materials and resources into a synthesized form, and then, to the occupation of people and goods that provide aid services. From start to finish, the intention of the gift must be respected as each party literally takes and gives the gift: accepting receipt of it, transforming it and passing it along. As a result of this exchange, the implemented gift is necessarily an inexact manifestation of the original objective.

With each phase there is also a dynamic of give and take with the gift's content. As its intended effect is converted, within the limits of the medium from its received to new phase, information is gained and lost, possibly diminishing or enriching the character of the gift. Every exchange is also a give and take negotiation. To secure a commitment that the gift will be transferred in the spirit of its stated purpose, the handling parties' economic or social interest must be met. They determine what value is to be extracted from the gift and agree upon that to be added to contribute to the gift's further exchangeability.

Architecture is a good example of the complex dynamic of giving. Architects translate the concurrent and typically competing desires of a given commission into a comprehensive action plan. The plan covers oversight, management and execution, and conveys an agreed upon intent and outcome. An essential part of the creative process is to design for and then respond to the give and take that occurs in all phases of translation of the plan into the final form. Detailed specifications for each phase are drafted into the plan, taking into account all the possible conditions that potentially diminish or enhance its execution. Like that of a gift, the path followed to carry out a project lies within a fluid matrix of limitations, resources and agreements whose fluctuations impact the favorability of the project's outcome. Once the project is underway, the architect must then capitalize on the actual dynamic conditions that arise in global markets and in the field so as to enrich the plan's intent. Like delivering a gift, realizing a building necessitates moving through this gauntlet of opening and closing opportunities—transforming the project's original meaning by in some instances giving in and reducing the extent of some its attributes, while in others taking advantage of the circumstances to enrich its composition.

Finally, like architecture, the process of giving necessitates welcoming the opportunities that crop up at each step with a willingness to expose the gift's intention to forces that can increase its capacity. At the same time, however, it requires safeguarding its integrity through the process and recognizing the point at which such enforcement needs to be relinquished. The gift's function will inevitably transform after its delivery, departing from its original objective as the received gift is used and its potential fulfilled. In other words, managing aid involves generously removing oneself from the equation at some moments and exercising close control in others. Which one to apply and to what degree is the art of give and take that ultimately determines the effectiveness of delivery. Rather than the locus of its greatest challenges, management is potentially Aid Capital's primary asset.

The practice of giving thus entails accepting its approximate and indeterminate nature as much as its omnipresence. Importantly, it involves understanding that one receives the most from it by embracing the art of its exchange. The aesthetics of giving, the give and take of every interaction that leads to a gift's greatest realization, is a form of Aid Capital that bears gifts to those who enter into the World of Giving.

Why Give?

While giving is considered an act of generosity providing some form of benefit to others, it is complicated by the fact that benefit also flows to the giver. An act of giving can, consciously or not, yield reward to the giver in the form of public recognition, professional or social advancement, spiritual satisfaction, monetary gain, etc. Thus, underneath a sincere intention to do good are complex and sometimes contradictory motivations. For instance, the wish to contribute time or money to effect a positive social result for others may coexist with another desire for the contribution to provide the giver with useful social networking. In that sense, giving is a form of exchange where the giver both gives and receives.

Four terms chart the basic motives to give: altruism, duty, self-interest and reciprocity. These concepts will serve as reference points to map the complex network of motivations at play in every situation of giving. While terms such as altruism and self-interest may seem polarized or in irresolvable conflict, their interrelation will instead unfold the gift's dynamic potentials. The rewards accepted by the giver, as well as the recipient, are an inherent part of giving, rather than something which a prospective giver might fret over or feel shame. Pragmatic analyses of giving, with eyes wide open, can result in better-considered decisions whose calculations consciously resolve intentions and weigh the outcome for both the giver and recipient. An informed gift that results in a benefit to the giver need not diminish any positive outcome for the recipient. Above all, in the economy of giving, the variety of returns that flow back to the giver can encourage further acts of giving.

Much of the time, the nature of the recipient group and the giver's relation to that group can impact motivations for giving. The recipient party can vary in size—from an individual stranger, to one's immediate family, to an extended kin-related network, to a close-knit set of individuals, to a group so numerous that no member knows all the others. The intended recipient may be a group as broad and abstract as the current and future population of humankind.

If an act of giving is never one of pure, absolute altruism, neither is it necessarily one of self-interest above all. Economists who have addressed the question of giving maintain that people only act to improve their own situation, basing analysis on the model of the "economic man"—one whose pursuit of satisfaction is only fulfilled through rational acts of self-interest. Similarly, some evolutionary biologists and psychologists suggest all animal and thus human behavior has emerged through successful self-preservation and, therefore, all acts, even the most seemingly altruistic, must ultimately be motivated by evolution's promotion and magnification of instinctual self-interest.

Still, there are plenty of examples of giving heavily weighted toward altruism—acts in the interest of the others' welfare with little immediate reward for the giver, such as the exhausting voluntary caretaking of someone with a mentally degenerative condition or sacrificing one's own safety to protect others. In the purest sense, absolute altruism may be an unobtainable ideal. Nonetheless, altruism remains a powerful internal motivation for giving in a complex constellation with other motivations: duty, reciprocity and self-interest.

Altruism

Altruism is at the heart of the tenets of most major world religions. Praise is bestowed upon those who give without the expectation of benefit, as in the Hindu proclamation:

> Giving simply because it is right to give, without thought of return, at a proper time, in proper circumstances, and to a worthy person, is enlightened giving. Giving with regrets or in the expectation of receiving some favor or of getting something in return, is selfish giving. (Bhagavad Gita 17.20–21)

Similarly, a passage from the Bible cites the virtue of giving without concern for one's own welfare.

> And he sat down opposite the treasury and watched the people putting money into the offering box. Many rich people put in large sums. And a poor widow came and put in two small copper coins, which make a penny. And he called his disciples to him and said to them, "Truly, I say to you, this poor widow has put in more than all those who are contributing to the offering box. For they all contributed out of their abundance, but she out of her poverty has put in everything she had, all she had to live on. (Mark: 12:41–44)

Buddhist teachings also reinforce the altruistic idea of selflessness when acting in the interest of others.

> Enlightening beings are magnanimous givers, bestowing whatever they have with equanimity, without regret, without hoping for reward, without seeking honor, without coveting material benefits, but only to rescue and safeguard all living beings. (Garland Sutra 21)

In articulating ethical laws to live by, British philosopher David Hume (1711–1776) claims that humans are fundamentally altruistic. Although individuals may be influenced by motivations that range across a spectrum of benevolence and self-interest, Hume maintains that benevolence is the dominant tendency. The alternative to self-interest is not indifference, but, according to Hume, a natural sympathy that people have for the happiness of others, a characteristic rooted in an individual's recognition of the importance of general social welfare.[1]

A century after Hume, Darwin's theory would seem to have little room for actions that benefit others while risking an individual's own survival and reproductive viability.[2] However, a Vervet monkey may sound out an alarm call upon perceiving a predator nearby, drawing the predator's attention, while simultaneously providing the other troop members with crucial moments to hide or flee. The chances of survival for the alarm-sounding monkey are greatly diminished while the ability of the ones that remain silent improves. Why then doesn't this Vervet alarm-altruism simply cease to exist, unfavorable for an organism's survival, eliminated by the process of natural selection? A troop in which such a tendency for sounding alarm was entirely absent would be less reproductively fit overall than one with the occasional few who inherit and also manifest a tendency to call alarm from time to time. The siblings of the alarmist monkey are more likely to survive and may carry variants of the genetic tendency to sound alarm. The gene's continuing circulation in the genetic pool of the species would be crucial for the troop's and the evolving species' overall survival. A troop that includes some true altruists is more likely to survive than ones consisting exclusively of selfish monkeys.

Given this reconciliation of altruism with Darwinian logic, can the principle of natural selection serve as an explanation for all acts of human altruism? While biological altruism might be said to apply to human beings, self-sacrifice also occurs among organisms that are likely incapable of making conscious decisions such as ants who remain outside the entrance of their colony and seal the hole from night predators, thereby consigning themselves as likely prey. Other ants climb to the roof of a tunnel, grasp hold and morph into honeypots, forever immobile, as a source of liquid sustenance for the others busy at work. By contrast, human beings consciously decide whether or not to act unselfishly. However, implemented actions may be based on erroneous assumptions and may not necessarily result in improving the fitness of the group or community. In other words, we can choose to act altruistically in addition to the influences of any instinctual altruism, though this is no guarantee of outcome.

Altruistic giving remains a challenging topic for economists. Such giving is considered counter to their basic models—simply uneconomic. Assuming a person makes rational choices about relinquishing the possession of a scarce resource (like money or time), he/she will decide to exchange that resource for something of optimum use or reward. Following this logic, it's irrational for a person to decide to just give away money earned by expending time and energy without expecting something of value in return. The giver must expect that the gift indeed provides a benefit. Economists quantify this benefit as a value or utility—which in this case would be the relative economic improvement to the receiver brought about by the gift.

The concept of utility helps to model other factors influencing the altruist's disposition to give. For example, theories vary on the role distance plays. British economist Francis Ysidro Edgeworth (1845–1926) argued that the greater the social or physical distance between giver and receiver, the greater difficulty there is to determine the receiver's increase in utility to the giver as a result of the gift. With less knowledge of likely benefit the desire to give decreases.

Edgeworth's Theory of Distance

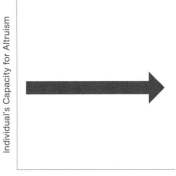

Individual's Capacity for Altruism

Geographic Distance from Other

It is easier for an individual to possess knowledge of another's utility function, and in turn act altruistically toward a recipient, when there is considered human interaction observed among members in a close-knit group. But economists have had difficulty explaining altruistic acts when the giver and recipient do not share such ties. It doesn't explain for example, why an individual decides to give to an unknown person residing 6000 kilometers away. Phillipe Fontaine, a contemporary French economist working on the subject of altruism and philanthropy, proposes that we reconsider empathy as the reason an individual can grasp another's utility to form a capacity for altruism—regardless of degree of familiarity or physical distance.[3]

Fontaine's Theory of Altruism

Individual's Capacity for Altruism

Geographic Distance from Other

An individual may also be willing to cooperate with strangers. Cooperation can indicate a willingness to act for the sake of a greater collective good. Cooperative behavior often occurs between members of family or close-knit groups, but it can also be initiated and established among people unacquainted with one another. Cooperation that results in perceivable benefits to both parties can increase and maintain itself over time. Individuals may demonstrate a commitment to sustain a mutually beneficial cooperative social economy to such a degree that they will do so at a personal cost. Yet, cooperative arrangements may be maintained by force by those who benefit most within a group against those who suffer the greatest cost and no longer wish to participate or who, instead, attempt to accrue benefits at cost to others.

Contracts must be capable of being enforced. Altruistic punishment enforces cooperation within a group by punishing those who takes advantage of the altruistic gestures of others. The group administers punishment against the swindler. By doing so, the group develops a surplus of trust that functions as a guarantee for the giver in future acts of altruism, reducing the likelihood of members taking untoward advantage of altruistic behavior.

Ability to Punish Non-Norm Conforming Behavior For The Public Good

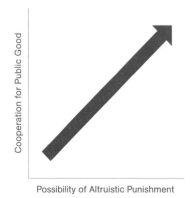

Cooperation for Public Good

Possibility of Altruistic Punishment

A 2003 study by a team of economists and psychologists—Gintis, et al.—shows that individuals will punish those who abuse the cooperative goodwill of others even when it brings no personal direct benefit. The study found that in situations where punishment could be used to enforce commitments, altruism and cooperation increased.[4]

In situations where punishment could not be used, cooperation and giving decreased. Participants, who did not know and did not communicate with each other were given monetary units to invest in a group project. Each determined their contribution and the total sum determined the return on the investment, to be divvied up equally among the participants. The more contributed, the greater the end reward for all. However, those who might give generously were at risk that free riders would invest very little and reap benefits at little danger to themselves. In some instances there was no ability to punish the free riders when it was revealed that they had contributed little overall. When the group became aware of the free riders, but had no means of remedy available, generosity decreased upon repeating the exercise. Where generous givers could punish free riders with a fine taken from the misers' own coffers—lowering the group's overall available funds for possible investment and thus their own potential return—the overall generosity increased. The self-sacrifice of altruistic punishment improved overall cooperation.

Duty

Duty imposes the impetus of external obligation upon an individual. Duty may be formalized through a commitment made to one's family, an oath sworn on behalf of one's community, a pledge taken to uphold a religious doctrine, or a set of laws or an ethical code. All of these might motivate one to give.

Gift-centered value systems embraced by an individual may explicitly specify recipient groups. For example, duty to give may apply only to one's family, affiliated group (a religious body, community organization or nation), those in dire need or all mankind. Jesus Christ is said by Christian doctrine to have washed the dusty feet of his disciples as a sign of the duty one has to another, regardless of rank.

Some philosophers consider giving to others a duty and part of a larger ethical imperative that must be obeyed, rather than an essential, inborn human trait. However, their views vary on the purpose of one's obligation to others.

In his *Two Treatises of Government*, John Locke (1632–1704) discusses an individual's duty to charity. For Locke, individuals have rights independent of the laws governing any given society. Stemming from these "natural" rights is an obligation to duties that serve one another—of upmost importance is that of charity.

According to Immanuel Kant (1724–1804), all individuals possess a will to do good. Good will is when a person consciously chooses to act in a morally worthy way, exclusive of other motivations. In that sense, Kant regarded it as a duty, or a self-imposed obligation, to take possession of one's good will and act upon it.

In John Stuart Mill's (1806–1873) view, an individual has the duty to take actions that promote the greatest overall amount of good or pleasure for others as well as for oneself. He argues that the principle of utility supersedes all other principles, as "actions are right in proportion to their promotion of happiness, and wrong as they produce the reverse."[5] This ideology creates an ethic of beneficence, where the purposefulness of all actions are judged according to their degree of improvement to the state of humankind.

Contemporary political philosophers addressing international justice argue for a more urgent, temporally bound sense of moral duty. Peter Singer (1946–present) asserts that it is an individual's duty to prevent as much suffering as possible, short of resulting in the giver being worse off than the recipient.[6]

While he acknowledges the extreme challenges such an applied ethics poses, he maintains that not giving to relieve recognized hardship is immoral.

Most religions view charity as a duty, and there are varied ways by which it is encouraged and compelled. In some instances, charity is described as a duty to a divine power, while in others it is said to be a moral duty in the pursuit of justice.

> We are commanded to give charity in accordance with our means and are forbidden to ignore the needs of the poor. (Judaism, 247:1)

> …and tell them that Allah has made obligatory on them a charity that is taken from their rich and given to their poor… (Islam, Reported by Bukhari and Muslim)

> For this is not for the ease of others and for your affliction, but by way of equality—at this present time your abundance being a supply for their want, that their abundance also may become a supply for your want, that there may be equality… (Christianity, II Corinthians 8:13–14)

In addition to the duty to give to those in need, some religions require contributions from practitioners in support of the maintenance of the religion's infrastructure, both human and material. The medieval tithe demanded a portion of one's income, while practices of animal sacrifice might ensure a meal for the clerics who presided over the ceremony.

Unlike philosophers and theologians who view duty as a moral imperative, economists view duty as an obligation imposed by the expectations and examples set by others in one's community. In other words, peer pressure can manifest as solemn duty. As well, if an individual is aware that others give, then the individual will be motivated to give to maintain one's social status, to be—at least—like everyone else.

An individual's duty to give is positively influenced by the gifts of peers and coworkers.

Gifts of Peers

Self-Interest

Individuals act out of self-interest when they consider their own needs above those of others. In the context of giving, this manifests as a gift ultimately, if not baldly, provided for the giver's own self-advancement. In other words, one is motivated to give in order to improve one's own conditions and capacities. At its extreme, this would be done in disregard for and at the expense of the welfare of others.

While religious doctrines admonish self-interested behavior as a sure path to damnation, other disciplines and philosophies have regarded self-interest as a natural component of human nature. Still others see self-interest as indicative of a heightened sense of self-awareness.

Some evolutionary psychologists argue that public acts of giving are a means for individuals to build a positive reputation among group members and thereby gain privilege and access to resources. One study (Bereczkei, Birkas and Kerekes, 2006) found that an individual was much more likely to give to an unknown recipient if his or her act of generosity was witnessed by peers. These researchers argue that public giving signals one's ability to cooperate and act as a valuable member of a group. When individuals gave in front of their peers, they were perceived as trustworthy, sympathetic and community-minded.

If

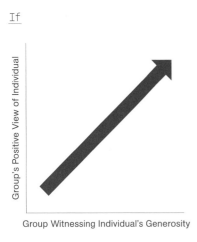

Group Witnessing Individual's Generosity

Then

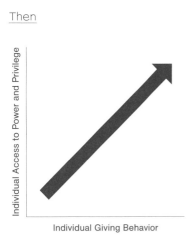

Individual Giving Behavior

Economists further reconcile giving's uneconomic nature and in particular any disadvantageous imbalance of the gift's transaction with the theory that donors give in order to achieve a warm glow. The satisfaction derived from the warm glow overcomes any material loss associated with prioritizing the needs of others over one's own. This contradicts the economic logic that one exchanges an item of value for something of equal (monetary) value. It is, for an economist, entirely irrational. Competitive giving describes individuals who desire to be perceived as more benevolent and trustworthy than their peers, as well as to feel as though they are making a difference. This is contradicted by the free-rider, who exploits others' pursuit of the warm glow. The warm glow may be that of one's own selfhood affirmed, an act of giving demonstrating that one's individual existence matters, in that it can have some impact on the world. A person might donate money to an organization that purports to protect dolphins, whether or not the person has been provided with proof of the organization's efficacy, but upon parting with a donation, will feel a warm glow while imagining its effect.

Competitive Giving/Warm Glow

Individual's Gift

Gifts from Others

Individual's Gift

Gifts from Others

Some philosophers argue that human nature is fundamentally self-interested. Both Thomas Hobbes (1588–1679) and Adam Smith (1723–1790) assert that self-interest dictates all human action. Hobbes views it as the satisfaction of internal desires. Even upon giving money to a beggar, Hobbes claims that he gave in order to feel better about his own status relative to the downtrodden nature of the individual in need. Smith claims that individuals must appeal to the self-interest of others in order to fulfill their own needs. "It is not from the benevolence of the butcher, the brewer, or the baker that we expect our dinner, but from their regard to their own interest. We address ourselves, not to their humanity, but to their self-love, and never talk to them of our own necessities, but of their advantages."[7]

Giving that is initiated out of self-interest, such as an increase in social status or an improved public image, may not incur an expense or harm to others. Instead, it may serendipitously have a positive impact on other's welfare. The total effect of the donation then remains positive.

Reciprocity

Reciprocity describes the motivation to give with the expectation that giving will result in a gift in return. This expectation might arise from an explicit arrangement with the recipient (as in, "I'll give you A, if you give me B"). The reciprocated gift could also be general and open-ended, as in doing a favor for someone with the expectation that an as-yet-to-be defined favor will be returned at some point in the future.

In many instances, the reciprocated gesture or reward, as in the case of a whispered thanks, is merely symbolic and of marginal exchange value with respect to the exchange value of the gift. Certainly, one may be persuaded to contribute a bit more to a cause in order to receive a fancier prize—the pledge amount to a public radio station for an enticing Monet water lilies umbrella may require double the sum which merely promises the station's mundane tote bag.

However, in most scenarios of giving, the giver understands that what they receive in return will in no way equal the value to the donation they make and gives nevertheless. The giver is not motivated because of an expectation of something in return of equal monetary or other value. The reciprocated gift acts simply as an incentive to donate to a cause; it is not the sole motivation to enter into the exchange. In order to be persuaded by a gift of little exchange value, the giver must to some extent already be invested in the gift's purpose or cause.

Reciprocity can be formalized to such an extent that a gift recipient's expected or required reciprocation can far exceed the value of the gift itself. In the highly influential text, *The Gift: The Form and Reason for Exchange in Archaic Societies*,[8] Marcel Mauss (1872–1950) describes gift exchange as a practice for building strong social ties among individuals of a group. In this case, the receiver of a gift is obligated to provide an offering of comparable material value. Moreover, the practice of reciprocation can become so socially important that the value accorded to the very act of passing the gift along to another in the group can exceed the object's material, or even spiritual, value. The receipt of such a gift immediately endangers the recipient who must not violate the sacred circulation of the gift.

Aided Altruism

Self-interested giving doesn't necessarily result exclusively in self-advancement and may, regardless of the giver's motives, positively impact a recipient. On the other hand, altruistic giving may enhance the welfare of others, yet, not incur a disabling or even significant cost for the giver.

Aided altruism reconciles the various factors leading to an act of giving. Like altruism itself, aided altruism involves the motivation to improve the welfare of others. The aided altruist's primary concern is for public good, to first and foremost give to others, while also appreciating that the satisfaction one gains from giving can be as great or greater than the gift itself. The aided encouragement of a benefit reinforces the motivation to give.

This return on one's gift, the motivation to give again, is one example of what we call Aid Capital. Aid Capital is the dynamic sum of one's capacity to give.

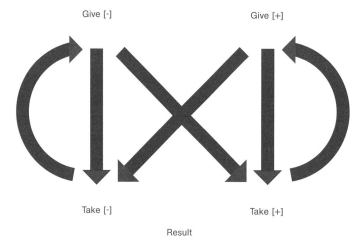

Motivation

Give [-]   Give [+]

Take [-]   Take [+]

Result

Strengthened motivation as a return on a gift is one possible qualitative measure of an actual increase in one's capacity to give—in one's Aid Capital. There are many means of increasing the total capacity to give, including the gift's own power not only to alleviate a lack, but also to provide the recipient with the capacity to potentially share the gift and help others. Acts of giving only occur in the presence of Aid Capital; acts of giving create Aid Capital. Acts of giving can grow Aid Capital in predictable and unpredictable ways, in all directions, for the giver, for the recipient, for those who facilitate the transaction along the way, both materially and motivationally. There is no limit to how much Aid Capital might be accrued, exponentially, worldwide.

Aided altruism recognizes that there are competing and complex forces at play in giving, requiring a more pragmatic model than one in which the degree of self-sacrifice is the only measure of the value of a gift. The gift's effect on others, rather than the cost to the giver, might be another measure. Time and resources allocated to effective channels of informational feedback to monitor the gift's arrival and impact may be regarded as equal in value to the time and resources allocated toward the preparation and transport of the gift.

Aided altruism operates under the belief that in order to improve the welfare of others it is not necessary to minimize or suppress one's own satisfaction when giving. If our aim is to materialize worthwhile support for others, then increasing the Aid Capital of a giver through reward makes sense. The rewards can range from lauds and public honor to a thank-you. Rewards could include a report that chronicles the positive impact of a gift over time. The aided altruist is the mega-donor who funds the new athletic facility in his or her own name, the recent graduate who volunteers in order to build contacts and the donor who feels good to have given to a worthy cause.

Public goods are what a giver provides through charitable giving. Recipients do not have to compete for these public goods and they are also not excluded from receiving them if they are unable to pay for them. In contrast, private goods are those that individuals compete for and consume as desired. Aided altruism acknowledges the distinct realms of public goods and private goods and assumes that the two areas of interest are not exclusive or necessarily in conflict.

Public Good = Altruistic Motive + Non-rival + Non-excludable

Private Good = Self-interested Motive + Rival + Excludable

Anonymous donations further complicate economists' assertions regarding the self-serving motivations behind charitable giving. The act of giving anonymously generates no accolades or public praise, but is still likely to provide a return, from the comfort of the warm glow to the satisfaction of watching the material effects of one's gift, whether that effect be the construction of a building, the expansion of a struggling organization, or the confidence provided by a gently used professional outfit. Though anonymous donations account for less than one percent of all private philanthropic gifts in the US, they are often very large in amount. Gifts by anonymous donors account for millions of dollars received by museums and universities.

Psychologists have defined two variables of personality, which help to inform differing degrees of satisfaction an individual gains from giving. The Edwards Personal Preference Schedule (Edwards, 1953) is one of several personality tests that seek to classify individuals based on ratios of various commonly held traits. The EPPS measures fifteen aspects of personality, defining relatively strong and weak motivations. Two of these characteristics, nurturance (the need to give) and succorance (the need to receive), suggest a Giving Personality. When the two characteristics are tested against one another (Ribal, 1962), four major giving personalities emerge:

Giving Personalities

The Altruistic Self
One who has a high motivational need to give and a low motivational need to receive.

The Selfish Self
One who has a low need to give and a high need to receive.

The Receptive-Giving Self
One who has a high need to both give and receive.

The Inner-Sustaining Self
One who has a low need to both give and receive.

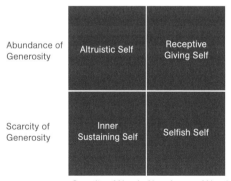

Pure altruism is arguably very rare. An individual who exhibits pure altruism only cares about the production of public good by the act of giving—not the consumption of private good. Like the pure altruist, the aided altruist cares about providing public good. This remains the primary motivation for giving. At the same time, the aided altruist is not indifferent to the rewards of giving. These rewards can consist of acquired job skills, organizational skills, social enrichment or advancement and new knowledge about the ways of the world. For the aided altruist, both the provision of public good and the rewards of giving factor into one's decision to give.

Potential givers can overcome doubt and hesitation as to the purity of their own motivations when prepared with an understanding of the dynamic factors that generate acts of giving. As well, informed potential givers can make well-considered—rather than impulsive—decisions as to what kind of gift to give, to whom the gift might be given and how to best utilize the available channels facilitating flows both from and to the giver. The potential giver should enjoy the process of research and consultation and should appreciate the increasing savvy and familiarity acquired after giving once, twice, again. The potential giver should look forward to directly touching the life of another human being—certainly the recipient of the intended gift—but also those lives touched by that recipient. There are also the yet-to-be-met potential givers with whom you will share your accumulated wisdom, one aspect of your reserve of expanding Aid Capital that only grows as it is given away.

3
History

Formalizations of Giving

Giving has occurred throughout human history in such activities as the sharing of food, collaboration of labor and communal childcare. Particular modes or techniques of giving have become ritualized, standardized and habitual. Formalized transfers of value and capacity include particular inheritance structures in which one generation gives the subsequent generation its accumulated property, dividing it among offspring or passing it in a single parcel to one privileged descendant, such as the first-born son. Where systems of public welfare have been adopted, the community regiments and formalizes the provision of assistance to members without adequate means to supply themselves with what is deemed to be life's bare necessities. Philanthropic foundations emerged with great concentrations of wealth in the hands of few industrial leaders. Unlike welfare, philanthropy provides for the transfer of funds to organizations that utilize the philanthropic gifts for the creation of institutions of self-improvement and education, thus giving the needy not immediate food or shelter, but instead a means to take advantage of the opportunities already available to their fellow citizens.

In the twentieth century, two previously informal modes of giving became institutionalized: the provision of international aid and the founding of governments based on the principles of communism. As the twentieth century drew to a close, another emerged, as users of digital media found that the technological capabilities of the internet allowed them to share works with each other in ways that defied long-standing notions of private and intellectual property. This last manifestation of a particular kind of culture of giving has resisted rigid management or institutionalization, due to the centerless operations of its very channels of transfer and exchange.

Inheritance

Improvisations of primogeniture in Tokugawa Japan show a pattern of giving in which family legacies were managed with greater concern for the family fortune than for purity of bloodlines. The basic unit of Japanese society, since the late eleventh century decline of the clan, had been the smaller and simpler *ie* (household or *messuage*) answerable to lords much as in Europe.[1] Taxes paid upwards bought "user rights" for the *ie*, which subsisted on rice cultivation.[2] Taxable property value at this time was actually measured in units of rice output, not geometrical area, thereby closely and very literally binding each family and individual to the productivity of the land.[3]

Changes in family structure thus had profound repercussions. A significant reformulation of the *ie* transpired in the late sixteenth century, when a new wife, instead of adopting her husband into her existing family, became absorbed into her husband's family.[4] This custom supported the acceptance of patrilineal succession with the eldest male son assumed to automatically ascend to the head of the household upon the death of the patriarch, preventing the fragmentation or endless division of the *ie*'s assets.

The right of primogeniture—the practice by which the eldest son acts as the sole inheritor of his family's assets—has been common to a diverse array of world cultures (a 1559 treatise authored by French humanist-politician Andreas Tiraquellus even draws a comparison between this culture of giving to the animal habit of feeding the eldest young first).[5] But it was during the Edo period of Japan (1603–1868), as feudal land relations were being subverted by the emergence of a commodity-based economy, that primogeniture took an unusual form. In the feudal system, the bloodline was organically linked to its land over generations. In the commodity economy, however, the careful maintenance and growth of the family's amassed wealth took priority, with the family assets treasured above genealogy, and guarded into the future from the mis-management of any less-than-brilliant offspring.

Primogeniture was made official in 1671 as a part of the Tokugawa government's effort to prevent the division of lands among non-heirs. Increasingly segmented family farms divided among offspring had the tendency to reduce and fragment the tax base from which ruling lords drew their power.[6] Japanese feudal estates were not centralized around the lord's residence as they were in Europe, but instead portioned across large territories and intermingled with other lords' holdings. Samurai were positioned as mediators between lords and peasants, to collect taxes and enforce law.

Succession in this time entailed not only the inheritance of land but also of various responsibilities to the family business, including managing legal contracts, labor and finances.[7] The fulfillment of the managerial duties associated with headship of family and business—felt strongly as an imperative to honor ancestral legacies—was often deemed so important that it could not be left to the chancy fate of primogeniture. An unprecedented culture of adoption arose to displace eldest sons who were judged unfit or unworthy. Paradoxically, to keep a family (as a business) strong, it was frequently found that the strength of the family (as a bloodline) must be compromised.

This pattern reached a peak in 1840, when more than one third of new heads were adopted and less than one half of new heads were eldest sons as imagined by the Tokugawa laws of primogeniture.[8] The pool of eligible heirs was not limited to a given family's extended kinship, but determined by criteria of merit. Recruits for adoption could force blood relations to be displaced from the ie.[9] In this light, adoption and designation as first-born seems to have been a subversion of law and tradition. Adoption of heirs by merit can be seen as a transformation of primogeniture into a social act of giving. From a legally enforceable inevitability, it became an opportunity to offer two gifts to whomever was found most worthy, not only of the family's wealth but also the family's trust.

Welfare

Welfare systems are instituted on the part of the state when the state assumes responsibility for its citizens' basic needs. For those who are unable to provide for themselves without such intervention, this system works to uphold minimum standards of health and safety. The success of welfare programs rests on a paradox. Welfare institutions must allow for both indiscriminate access—anyone with proof of citizenship is eligible to apply—and strict control of distribution of gifts according to an individual's need. This is determined by whether the citizen's need meets the predetermined threshold at which the state begins to give from its reserves collected through taxation of the entire populace.

One of the pioneering formalizations of welfare can be found in the predominately Calvinist Dutch Republic of the seventeenth and eighteenth centuries. As Europe's most prosperous state—with a monopoly on world trade, art and science—the Dutch Republic fostered a culture of restraint and seeming selflessness in asset allocation.[10] Both individuals and institutions were careful to keep expenditures below profits. Such frugality-within-wealth, described and analyzed by Max Weber in his 1904 sociological treatise *The Protestant Ethic and the Spirit of Capitalism*,[11] purchased a long-term social stability uncharacteristic of other free market economies, reliant on loans and debt to fuel their economies.

Profits not invested in capital improvements to manufacturing and shipping were regularly recycled into charitable institutions as investments in the future, a safety net woven for the entire population. As suggested by Weber, religious duty and what Michele Vovelle has aptly termed the "barometer of piety" motivated giving.[12] Those Calvinists who had amassed enough profit to spare provided indisputable proof of their state of grace, their predestined salvation and their eternally bankable divine favor. Giving demonstrated such a state of grace to themselves, to the general public and also to potential business partners and investors.

Though the incentivizing of giving by the promise of salvation of the dead disappeared with Catholicism after the Dutch revolt against Spain (1589–1648), the climate of religious tolerance that followed afforded an array of strategies, represented not only by the majority Calvinists, but also Lutherans, Mennonites and Jews.[13] These groups worked to care for "their own" in order not to lose them to another camp and targeted all socioeconomic groups: public alms boxes for the poor, compulsory giving during services and political pressure on the wealthy for larger contributions. The welfare of the populace benefitted from such competition and from the high stakes contests of charitable giving among business leaders as proof of God's favor.

This extent of control and stability was particularly impressive to travelers in comparison with much of the rest of urban Europe, throughout which beggars— teeming in crowds exceeding twenty thousand—made streets unsafe by day and night. Howell, a contemporary from Wales, observed of Amsterdam:

> It is a rare thing to meet with a beggar here, as rare as to see a horse, they say, upon the streets of Venice. And this is held to be one of their best pieces of government, for besides the strictness of their laws against mendicants, they have hospitals of all sorts for young and old, both for the relief of one and the employment of the other, so that there is no object here to exercise any act of charity upon.[14]

The republic ruled fiercely against opportunism (see *Chapter 2, Ability to Punish Non-Norm Conforming Behavior For The Public Good*). Anyone daring enough to attempt to cheat the welfare system met with harsh punishment. As those holding public office refrained from abuses of power for personal profit, citizens demonstrated a willingness to tolerate heavy taxes for the sake of the common good.[15]

Welfare projects included a *Weeshuis* for the education of orphans and poor children, a facility for the mentally ill and hospitals for wounded soldiers and impoverished pilgrims. Englishman John Evelyn remarked of these that, "indeed, it is most remarkable what provisions are here made and maintained for public and charitable purposes, and to protect the poor from misery…"[16] The quality of care a given group received in this society was directly related to the degree to which it could be perceived as innocent.[17] Orphanages, for example, whose subjects could be blamed for nothing, boasted provisions comparable to those enjoyed by the upper *burgerij*—which far exceeded needs of base subsistence. Even in leaner years, the orphans' diet included expensive meat and dairy, with regents reducing the quantity, but never the quality, of the food dispensed.[18]

From 1589 to 1621, twelve workhouses opened across the Dutch Republic, extracting labor and profits from individuals considered unemployable. Many of those dependent on welfare who subsequently entered the workforce had been well prepared by administrators who felt that, regardless of profit, labor was a healthful and healing activity.[19]

Generally, a spirit of goodwill and agreement about the treatment of those in need across institutions public, religious and private, jointly conspired to fashion a welfare society considered highly effective in its time.

Philanthropy

During the United States' Gilded Age, wealth rapidly concentrated and amassed among the new manufacturing and financial elite. An ethic of philanthropic support of cultural institutions began to dominate giving. The spirituality that had long underpinned charitable activity in the West, with emphasis on relief of *symptoms* of social inequities, was simply overwhelmed by the magnitude of new philanthropic foundations' programs to selectively amend the *lack of opportunity* it saw as the cause of underclass suffering.[20]

Galvanized by a self-righteous social Darwinism, oil, steel and financial tycoons performed a deft slight-of-hand with their religious heritage—refuting the idealization of poverty that had been so central to Judeo-Christian tradition, instead attributing it to moral ineptitude or rationalizing it as punishment for personal shortcomings.[21] Any sympathetic sentimentality was disdainfully dismissed. Biblical foundations for such a competitive attitude were presented as public evidence: "He becometh poor that dealeth with a slack hand, but the hand of the diligent maketh rich."[22]

In lieu of contributing to existing ideologically defined institutions such as the church, newly constituted, industrial-sized foundations saw an opportunity to shape a new realm of cultural influence. The Carnegie Institute's inaugural project was a rewrite of national economic history in 1902, explicit in its "reconciliation of private wealth with public welfare."[23] Select intellectuals were positioned as mediators between the elite and working classes, asserting capitalist ideologies as protective measures against the specter of socialism.

Framed by markets of exchange, philanthropy became legible as a hyper-luxury. Consumptive spending alone has a limit condition which, when approached, yields diminished returns. The gross scalelessness of these elites' holdings existed on a plane of abstraction beyond standard economic logic. Philanthropy allowed for the avoidance of the mess of materiality (foodstuffs, for example, ameliorating symptoms) in favor of assistance as information packaging and distribution. The benefactors could impose on the masses their own vision of themselves, the individual as a hard core of aspiration who, if provided with the opportunity to learn, could raise himself above his condition. Giving should optimally induce and enable aspiration.

Andrew Carnegie's *Gospel of Wealth* (1889) included a list of the "best fields for philanthropy" in descending order of importance: universities, free libraries, hospitals, laboratories, public parks, meeting and concert halls, swimming baths, and lastly churches.[24] Gifts were administered by and filtered through large institutions modeled after the profit-generating structures of the corporations that funded them.

Help, thus, would come to those who could demonstrate their willingness to improve self and society with the kind of effort that reflected the vigor and corporate spirit of the philanthropic system. Rejection of top-down management ideals meant, as never before, exclusion from assistance and opportunity. Not until the aspiring individual climbs through the corporate-industrial hierarchy and becomes no less than a captain of industry himself, would or should the individual be accorded the esteem and value deserved by a Rockefeller or Morgan. Philanthropy had mastered a new level of politics.

The crisis of 1929 inspired an astonishing change of policy. In 1931, the Rockefeller Foundation's forty thousand USD grant to the American Association of Social Workers, to "educate public opinion regarding the fundamental importance of welfare work in the present government," were responsible for massive marches, protests, and riots demanding federal intervention.[25] Before the Depression, the idea of a public welfare state had been regarded as unjust, if not offensive.

Only when the need for massive government assistance became accepted as a moral imperative did the government begin to consider the programs of private philanthropy. The groundwork laid before the crash held strong. The New Deal adopted, among its relief efforts, the private philanthropists' technique of applying the gift-as-self-help, with an ambitious schedule of public works projects distributing government dollars on the basis of employment. The most expansive of these self-help initiatives was the Works Progress Administration, devoting seven billion USD to public buildings and infrastructures but also arts and education projects. Between 1935 and1943, its workforce numbered almost eight million, the largest employer in the country.

Aid

The irrevocably global scope of economic and national interests in the postwar period extended the reach of giving into international relations. With governments polarized by competitive economic structures, business leaders—captains of both industry and capital management—became integral to government decision-making. During the Cold War, memories of the power of the nation-as-streamlined-factory were still fresh and provided technological momentum. The importance of seamless internal cooperation between institutions of giving, government and business, was a truth unquestioned.

Government had grown into a powerful aid organization itself during the Great Depression. Governments provided assistance to aid foundations in the form of tax exemptions, and those foundations furthered government causes abroad.

Top decision-makers in government and non-government organizations were forthcoming about the extent of their collaboration. Charles Fahs, Director of the Rockefeller Foundation's Division of Humanities from 1950 to 1962, explained that "foreign policy is the promotion of our national interests abroad and aid is an integral part of foreign policy administration," adding that "there is no advantage in trying to separate aid policy from the rest of foreign policy."[26] President Truman, too, stressed the inseparability of politics and economics by claiming that totalitarian (read: communist) regimes "spread and grow in the evil soil of poverty and strife,"[27] leaving little room for equivocation on the assertiveness with which *Pax Americana* was to be pursued.

In response to the threat of Russian expansionism, George F. Kennan of the State Department elaborated a "long term, patient but firm and vigilant" policy of containment. Impressive allocations of US dollars were put to this end, all with free-market strings attached, including over 600 million USD to fulfill the directives of the 1947 Truman Doctrine and twelve billion USD to fund those of the Marshall Plan.[28] These projects were funded in part by private organizations like the Ford Foundation. The United States was especially anxious to demonstrate the value of free-market democracy to a constellation of nascent states rising from the post-colonial mess left by exhausted old world superpowers. The immediate need to bolster the economies and militaries of existing, friendly democracies after the war was soon eclipsed by this new imperative. A vacuum of economic and governmental know-how after the retreat of the colonial powers rendered many African, Asian and Latin American states vulnerable to corruption and chaos.

In this climate, "soft power" became the new paradigm. Philanthropic support of education, for example, could engineer consent more effectively than the threat of violence. In 1961, The Agency for International Development (USAID) sent experts of various fields to developing countries to provide technical assistance. The Congress for Cultural Freedom (CCF), founded in 1950 with the support of both the Central Intelligence Agency (CIA) and the private Ford Foundation, had already been more deliberate, fostering local anti-communist advocacy groups that concealed their connection to larger institutions.[29] The strategy of deploying aid as information (or information as aid)—whether labeled "advocacy," "activism" or "education"—had significant international effects when private-public partnership streamlined the pioneering experiments of the early twentieth century titans of philanthropy.

Communism

Communism's inversion of capitalism's prioritization of private property generates a radical re-conceptualization of the act of giving. The lack of private property mandated by communism does not preclude gift giving, but rather transforms giving from an occasional transaction to an ongoing society-wide collaboration. Legal, material possession is no longer a requirement for a giver, as giving ceases to primarily designate a transfer of property. The gift is released from ownership. Far from excluding the gift, communism can be understood as a state of unconditional and total giving, liberated from the rigidity of discrete exchange between rigidly specified subjects.

Charity, in its affirmation of class hierarchy, has no place in communism, and the assets of charitable institutions thus must be assimilated (or "inherited") along with other private properties as the raw materials to build the new state. Communist propaganda disparages individual giving as symptomatic of the hypocrisy of capitalism.[30] Communism represents itself as no longer relying on an exclusive elite to redistribute assets, but instead on a collective assumption of responsibility.

Before the October Revolution, Imperial Russian cultures of giving reflected a Byzantine belief that misery and suffering elevated the spirit, that poverty equated divinity and that charity was one of few sanctified paths. As Natalia Dinello explains, Russians attributed "sacredness neither to work nor money, but encourage[d] unconditional sharing."[31] Mores of mutual support afforded Russians a steadfast solidarity.

Konstantin Aksakov described his nation as a harmonious whole favoring *obshchina* (community) over selfish individualism.[32]

The prophesies of the philosopher Hegel—self-realization of the spirit, human freedom, heightened consciousness all formalized in the perfect state—were appealing to Russian intellectuals, but the decidedly western rationality and individuality Hegel identified as engines of progress proved incompatible. In Russia the concept of land was not so much a legal device as a "moral and spiritual agreement."[33] The deftest of Russian thinkers appropriated dialectics to argue, against Hegel's eurocentrism, a uniquely eastern state of historical maturity, of fraternity and selflessness.

This context accounts for the gusto with which Russians received Marxist criticisms of the egoistic Protestant ethic of the West. In a letter to Marx that could well have been written by any number of Russian intellectuals, Engels complains that:

> Darwin did not know what a bitter satire he wrote on mankind, and especially on his countrymen, when he showed that free competition, the struggle for existence, which the economists celebrate as the highest historical achievement, is the normal state of the animal kingdom. Only conscious organization of social production can lift mankind above the rest of the animal world as regards the social aspect.[34]

The arrival of philosophical and scientific materialism in Russia, despite state censorship, had effected a miniature, and belated, Enlightenment in a culture otherwise estranged from positivist worldviews. The exciting image of a vast web of forces organizing the many "complex combinations of chemicals"[35] that constitute life was effectively extrapolated into the macro scale of society. The synthetic potential of the irrevocably inverse and reciprocal relations of cause and effect— along with the idealist tinge of materialism—together entered the realm of historical struggle and became the compromise later known as dialectical materialism.

Bolshevik rhetoric subsequently posited these themes in heavily political and industrial language. Matter, animated by perpetual *peredelka* (remaking), *perekovka* (re-forging) and *pereplavka* (remolding), was the unifying common denominator of class struggle.[36] Bolshevists were no longer concerned with the religious construct of evil, but rather with a radical departure from social construction of class.

Trotsky spoke hopefully of a "second edition"[37] of mankind, in an almost Lamarckian sense of social evolution toward the *übermensch*. Alexander Etkind writes of "The New Soviet Man" that he was "supposed to be fair and fearless; invulnerable to greed, pain, and love; ecstatic about the state and purged of private loyalties; unaware of his own mortality."[38] These qualities would be the foundation of a society of selflessness, of the unlimited gift. The individual would give himself as total gift to the solidarity and mutual love of the commonwealth. Any less would not suffice.

In order for such gift-giving to take place, two conditions must have already been met: collective ownership of means of production and the abolition of wage labor. With everyone sharing and working equally the same pool of resources, everyone is bound to the condition of the whole population. By abandoning the Darwinist struggle against one's fellows and struggling instead united and together, communist societies propose an economy not of acquisition and consumption, but of total and universalized giving. Given the precondition of selflessness in the new man, everyone gives everything to the state, which in turn is coincident with everyone—balancing the economy thus: all give all to all.

Sharing

Digital duplication assures that giving does not ne-
cessitate the loss of the given object on the part of the
giver. Neither is a gift restricted to a single recipient.
In fact, sharing can be nearly universal, with willful
dissolution of private property into the public domain.
Collaboration succeeds competition; as Kevin Kelly
says of what he calls the group-mind, "nobody is as
smart as everybody."[39]

While traditional economies, based on the production and consumption of material goods, are subject
to laws of finitude and scarcity and thus ascribe value
to exclusivity, economies of information, distinct in
their relatively low and continually decreasing material
costs, are structured by a logic in which value is directly
related to plenitude. As participation in global networks
and productive immersions in digital information surged
in the nineties, contagious informational generosity
became the prime currency of the Internet.[40]

The emergence of such potential for generosity
can be traced to the grassroots movements of the
1960s and the military advancement of communications technologies in the aftermath of World War II.
The youth counterculture of the 1960s was a project
in novel forms of community. Its explicit contestation
of capitalist property relations, apathetic conformity
and the nuclear family as the ideal unit of society found
its most salient expression in the establishment of
myriad communes. To various extents, private property
became assimilated into the shared material holdings
of the commune.

The ideological positioning of such projects was
frequently predicated on a spiritual oneness and
general feeling of the interconnectedness of phenom-
ena introduced to the west by eastern philosophies.
These imports often specifically endorsed detachment
from material possessions. The susceptibility of American youth to Buddhism and Hinduism in particular is
symptomatic of what Jung identified as a larger cultural

shift from the righteous approach to spirituality as way of perfecting the self to a more embracing spirituality-as-wholeness.[41]

The act of communication, central to any relational model, quickly became the focus of a parallel series of practices. Among the most successful sites for experiments in communication were Michael Murphy and Richard Price's Esalen Institute in Big Sur, California. Founded in 1962 as a "psychological spa" dedicated to the development of "new methods of personal and interpersonal relations," it operated a mixed schedule of guest speakers, seminars, workshops, and exercises such as eye-a-logues—the practice of two people staring at each other in silence—meant to circumvent society's "excessive verbalism." The Institute attracted the participation of as many as twenty-five thousand people per year, including personalities such as Aldous Huxley and Alan Watts.

Meanwhile, at the RAND Corporation, Olaf Helmer and Norman Dalkey were at work structuring an asynchronous cycle of anonymous feedback as a collaborative problem solving mechanism. At the Institute for Defense Analysis in the late sixties, Murray Turoff's research in teleconferencing for nuclear war planning led to a computational communication network based on the Delphi Method, Helmer's and Dalkey's paper-based predecessor of subsequent many-to-many communication technologies. In 1968, Doug Englebart's parallel efforts with his Augmentation Research Center achieved cult notoriety through a ninety-minute demonstration of live-integrated text, voice and video.[42]

Other studies in communal interchange include creative adaptations of more familiar formats, such as the printed catalogue. The *Whole Earth Catalogue*, the 1968 brainchild of Northern California intellectual and activist Stewart Brand, was a series of compendia of obscure, amateur D.I.Y. technologies assembled by its own user-group to facilitate their anti-corporate, ecologically sustainable living practices.[43] Without centralized authorship or regulation, the *Catalogue* provided a forum for expansive, multilateral conversation. The type of interaction engendered by the *Whole Earth Catalogue* was an empowering and democratic form of information collection and dissemination that Brand would extend through his next project, the Whole Earth 'Lectronic Link. Cofounded in 1985 with Larry Brilliant, the WELL effectively democratized the network technology previously known only to military elite.[44] With a dial-up modem, users in remote geographic locales could simultaneously engage in the decentralized sharing of opinions and data-files. Howard Rheingold has described this co-option of military technology by a grassroots medium as "the primordial ooze where the online community was born."[45]

Propelled by the cultural momentum of communalism, but suddenly unfettered from the weight of materiality, digitally decentralized social organizations were in a unique position to foster open systems of collaboration-through-appropriation, authorial creation and gift distribution—a technological realization of the communal ideologies and communications games of the sixties.

4
Capacities

Technical Glossary

Aid Activity
Projects and programs, cash transfers, deliveries of goods, training courses, research projects, debt relief operations and contributions to non-governmental organizations.

Aid Agency
An organization that focuses on distribution rather than collection of gifts. Aid agencies can be an arm of government, be inter-governmental or be an external, voluntary organization.

Concessionality Level
A measure of the "softness" of a credit reflecting the benefit to the borrower compared to a loan at market rate.

Bilateral
Aid flow channeled directly by a donor country to a recipient country.

Disbursement
The release of funds, including those for technical advice, or the purchase of goods or services for a recipient. They may be recorded gross (the total amount disbursed over a given accounting period) or net (the

gross amount less any repayments of loan principal or recoveries on grants received during the same period). It can take several years to disburse a commitment.

DAC (Development Assistance Committee)

A forum comprising most of the OECD members, set up to address poverty reduction and the economic welfare of developing countries. The World Bank, the IMF and UNDP also participate as observers.

Development Bank

A multilateral institution that addresses, in the form of grants and loans, the needs of developing countries. They make a varying portion of their capital in the global market.

FDI (Foreign Direct Investment)

The establishment of a business in a host economy by a foreigner, where the parent enterprise maintains controls over the local affiliate regardless of national boundaries. FDI is a profit-making or long-term investment and not a gift or a loan.

GDP (Gross Domestic Product)

The dollar value of all final goods and services produced within a country; a measure of a country's economy in a given year.

GNI (Gross National Income)
The dollar value produced within a country, varying subtly from the GDP. GNI includes the producer economy's income received from other hosting countries. For example, profits made by a US company operating in the UK will count towards UK GDP but US GNI.

IMF (International Monetary Fund)
A multilateral institution with 185 contributing member countries, providing technical assistance, temporary financing and economic policy advice to countries in order to stabilize global exchange rates and international payments. It has a macroeconomic focus.

Institution
A formalized, administrative entity with recognized clout, hierarchies of decision-making and projected stability over time.

LIC (Lower Income Country)
A class of countries designated to receive development aid; further delineations within LICs refer to specific relief programs and include NICs (Newly Industrialized Countries), HIPCs (Heavily Indebted Poor Countries) and LICUS (Low-Income Countries Under Stress).

Loans
Transfers for which repayment is required.

Multilateral
Aid flow channeled via an international
organization active in development .
Examples of multilaterals are the World Bank
or the UNDP.

MDG (Millennium Development Goals)
Drawn from the Millennium Declaration
of the United Nations' Millennium Summit
in September 2000 and accepted by 189
countries, the MDGs primarily aim for a fifty
percent reduction in the global poverty rate
by the year 2015.

Net Flow
The total amount disbursed over a given
accounting period, less repayments of loan
principal and not accounting for interest.

NGO (Non-Governmental Organization)
A voluntary, civil organization that is not
formally bound to the interests of the
political leaders of its home nation.
Generally, although not necessarily, they are
accorded tax-exempt or nonprofit status
and are organized around particular cultural,
ecological and social welfare agendas.

OA (Official Assistance)
Financial disbursements from a DAC member country or countries to one of the countries on the OECD's list of developing countries. According to OECD criteria, an OA recipient would not be one of the least developed countries.

ODA (Official Development Assistance)
A grant or a loan given to promote the economic development and social welfare of developing countries, including least developed countries. ODA loans include a grant element of at least twenty-five percent. They can either be bilateral (from government to government) or multilateral (via a central institution such as the World Bank).

ODF (Official Development Finance)
The measurement of the total inflow of resources to recipient countries. It includes bilateral ODA, grants and development lending by multilateral financial institutions and some development-related OOF.

OECD (Organization for Economic Co-operation and Development)
An international organization of thirty developed countries established in 1961 to promote free market economies and democratic governance. Its agenda includes

sustainable economic growth, support of world trade and the maintenance of stability in the international community. It has a tiered list of countries which merit financial assistance.

OOF (Other Official Flows)
Assistance and donations not aimed at development such as military assistance in the event of civil war.

Private Flows
Flows of aid at market terms financed out of private sector resources and private grants, such as those made by an NGO or other private body such as a religious organization or foundation.

Tied Aid
An official grant or loan where the goods or services must be procured in the donor country or a group of countries that does not include a substantial number of likely aid-recipient countries.

Technical Assistance
The provision of non-local knowledge, advice, expertise or training in order to improve procedures, implementation or policy.

UN (United Nations)

An intergovernmental association whose stated aims are to facilitate cooperation in international law, international security, economic development, social progress, human rights and achieving world peace. The UN was founded in 1945 after World War II to replace the League of Nations, to stop wars between countries and to provide a platform for dialogue. There are currently 192 member states, including nearly every recognized independent state in the world.

UNDP (United Nations Development Programme)

A network that provides advice, training and grant support to developing countries with the purpose of assisting the realization of the Millennium Development Goals.

UN-HABITAT (United Nations Human Settlements Programme)

A bureaucratic entity formed in 1978, charged by the UN member nations with advocating sustainable urban and rural living environments and promoting the notion of adequate shelter for all.

Untied Aid

ODA for which the associated goods and services may be fully and freely procured in all countries, often preferably in the recipient country.

WFP (World Food Programme)
The food aid branch of the United Nations and the world's largest humanitarian organization. The WFP operates five United Nations Humanitarian Response Depot (UNHRD) locations that maintain emergency relief supplies.

WHO (World Health Organization)
A United Nations agency that acts as a coordinating and policy authority on international public health.

World Bank
A multilateral institution comprised of two branches: the International Bank for Reconstruction and Development (IBRD) for middle-income and high-credit countries and the International Development Association (IDA) for the lowest-income countries. Focused on economic and human development, the Bank provides loans, credits and grants to developing countries for a wide array of purposes internally categorized as education, health, public administration, environmental and natural resource management, infrastructure development and agriculture.

Channels

Three primary channels direct capital flows across the international aid landscape: bilateral agencies, such as USAID; multilateral institutions such as the International Monetary Fund; and non-governmental organizations (NGOs) ranging from unnamed kitchen-table organizations of two people to international NGOs, such as World Vision with its staff of 40,000.[1] Although there exist some mechanisms that attempt to guide the distribution and allocation of aid funds, the scale and complexity of contemporary giving makes this an extremely difficult task, with only limited success thus far. No master global regulatory regime has been successfully established to reliably track flows and transformations as aid travels through and across channels, nor is there any means to absolutely guarantee the receipt of aid in the quantity and form intended by donors.

The relationship between donor and recipient has its own set of complications, and further, each channel has clear strengths and weaknesses dictated by its particular operational characteristics. The rise in coop-eration between public and private giving sectors has also brought about a host of challenges to the support and maintenance of efficient flow. Helmut Reisen of the Organization for Economic Co-operation and Develop-ment Center (OECD) recently stated: "One would like to think that the international aid architecture is an orderly process guided by simple principles, but the trends clearly show that we have a non-system…[that] does not result from coherent design, but is a child of spontaneous disorder."[2] The vast, multifarious network of channels is nonetheless linked in the most basic sense by a mission to provide relief and assist develop-ment. At the very least, a collaborative attitude would seem preferable to a hostile, combative one among the players, yet the lack of discrete accounting and clear control of the process—from initiation to receipt to implementation—can muddy aid's terrain.

Bilaterals and Multilaterals

Established by a central government, bilateral agencies are hierarchical in structure. This is generally positive in terms of accountability and budget responsibility, yet expertise held by subordinates is not necessarily put to best use. Multilateral institutions are largely hierarchical as well, albeit in a more cooperative sense than bilateral agencies; because they represent a host of donor countries, multilaterals are more efficient at pooling resources. The downside of multilateral distribution tends to be financial inefficiency. A significant percentage of the agency's funding is dedicated to administrative costs: accounting, allocation research and effectiveness studies.

Bilateral and multilateral funds, despite rigorous planning and subsequent observation, can still be delayed and by no means escape the risk of misappropriation en route. Increasingly, NGOs are employed as distributors, thus reducing the amount of time aid spends within the bilateral or multilateral channels. As a result, their role has been shifting from the massive deployment of aid itself to the selection of appropriate non-governmental partners with whom to collaborate.

Macro-level oversight for bilateral giving lies with the Organization for Economic Co-operation and Development (OECD), which monitors member countries' allocations through mutual examination, peer reviews and multilateral surveillance mechanisms. Official Development Assistance (ODA) is defined as bilateral funding designated solely for the developing countries on the Development Assistance Committee (DAC) list of recipients. However, this list of recipients, conventionally used to designate targets for aid, was originally intended as a means of directing and focusing attempts at the statistical tracking of aid flows, not to place absolute limits on where aid may flow.[3] Bilateral, or government, agencies ultimately have control when selecting recipients, yet the likelihood of reliable information about and feedback from familiar DAC-listed nations makes them tempting targets.

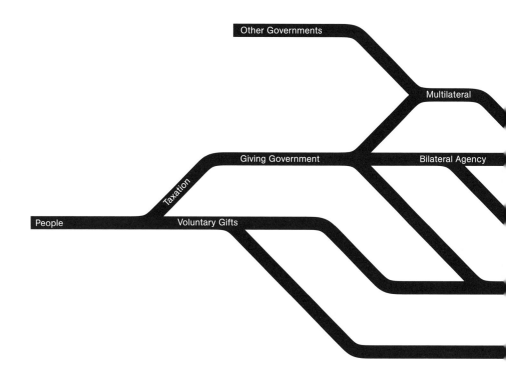

Other Governments

Multilateral

Giving Government

Bilateral Agency

Taxation

People

Voluntary Gifts

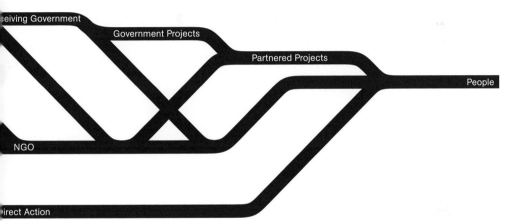

1975: 500 ECOSOC NGO's

1975: 25,000M USD in Private Capital Flows

1975: 10,000M USD in ODA Flows

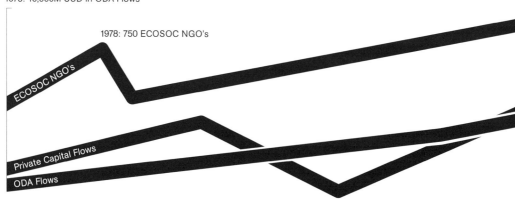

1978: 750 ECOSOC NGO's

ECOSOC NGO's

Private Capital Flows

ODA Flows

90

1975   1979   1983   1987

2007: 3,000 ECOSOC NGO's

2007: 350,000M USD
in Private Capital Flows

1996: 40,000M USD in Private Capital Flows

2007: 75,000M USD
in ODA Flows

2002: 10,000M USD in Private Capital Flows

| 1995 | 1999 | 2001 | 2007 |

An NGO is identified by what it is not—a Non-Governmental Organization. It was first defined as such by the United Nations in 1945 as a way to clarify and legitimize its dealings with organizations other than governments, and during a period of time when governments still occupied a privileged position in the collective imagination.

Individually, certain NGOs are arguably hardly non-governmental, in that they work closely with government agencies to achieve government aims or provide services in realms that are normatively considered to be the exclusive domain of governments, such as national healthcare. Even if adamantly outside of government machinery, many are focused on policy ("advocacy" from the NGO perspective) as the primary tool for achieving their goals, interacting with government by applying external pressure. Despite this closeness, NGOs' characteristics, roles and behaviors in the development and aid process are often described in the same way that they are defined: in opposition to government or any other centralized institutions that might be involved.

By and large, NGOs have proven to be a successful addition to the development and humanitarian aid field—for instance, many current sustainable practices were researched, developed, initiated and importantly, maintained through monitoring by NGOs.[6] Their successes, however are often credited to a projected idea of form—non-hierarchical (more in touch with beneficiaries, including an awareness of needs and wants), flexible (responsive), small (less susceptible to bureaucratic entanglements), informal (able to avoid the corrupt, misguided, or self-serving channels of government), direct (efficient) and externally-focused (resources and energy are not spent on organizational matters, so more reaches recipients). The resultant effect of this type of organization is meant to provide aid more quickly, more precisely, more effectively and with less funding lost to any administrative costs or overhead.

This purported smallness and directness is often positively evoked when discussing NGO/government/institutional collaborations. The contrast in forms allows for a cross-section of scales to be applied to meet needs, where each supplements and reinforces the other. Many NGOs are structured and operate in this way, but it can be in some sense dangerous to causally link form to performance. NGOs have brought to the aid landscape the benefit of depth—a plurality of organizational forms, not a rigid or stagnant type.

An organization may be small and lean, but the projects, or issues, rarely are. In any urban development project, for example, numerous, city, regional and national agencies are involved, from utilities and services to permits and zoning, in addition to private and commercial enterprises and participatory community organizations. This means that NGOs must almost always operate in concert with an array of other groups, also including cooperative and uncooperative NGOs. The frequent result of this interaction is an increase in complexity, leading to conflict, compromises, delays, information corruption and increases in cost.[7]

There can be concrete blockages to significant development posed by existing laws or territories of control, such that an NGO needs more than simply conviction and an idea in order to make changes. For example, Bangladesh is one of the poorer countries in the world and also one with a rapidly expanding urban area, Dhaka. As is frequently the case, exploding urban growth without comparable economic growth tends to strain infrastructure and housing resources and capabilities. In Dhaka, however, NGOs are limited in their capacity to effect urban development due to the government's jurisdiction over services; the Dhaka Water Supply Authority (DWASA) solely controlled access and billing without allowing any outside collaborative intervention until

Grameen Bank's founder, Muhammad Yunus, on a banner outside of Grammen's headquarters in Dhaka, Bangladesh.

recent losses from illegal connections forced them to reconsider. This made NGO slum sanitation efforts incredibly difficult to achieve at scale.[8]

Simply because a government is not attending to the conditions of every citizen, does not mean that it is open to others doing so. Further, Bangladesh's government has, in recent history, been one that has taken a regulatory attitude towards NGO activity, consistent to varying extents through all three governments since independence (Awami League, BNP and the Jatiya Party). Regulatory measures inherited from British rule and institutional means of control manifest in registration requirements and oversight agencies such as the Association of Development Agencies in Bangladesh (ADAB). Lastly, the government tends to hold a certain amount of financial control, through the ability to provide favorable loan terms to certain development agencies.[9] All NGOs operate under these conditions, not just those which overlap with government responsibility, which has resulted in accusations of government restriction of civil society despite the benefits of transparency such practices might provide.[10]

How does an organization collaborate with a government that is not fully cooperative to NGO advances without formal processing? How does an NGO work around or overcome these issues? A particular solution comes also from Bangladesh, one which displays adaptations of the normative NGO typology in an effort to operate within realistic conditions, as Bangladesh's situation is in no way unique in the developing or the developed world.

This instance of a working NGO solution actually appears to be nothing like an NGO. Two prominent examples, BRAC (Bangladesh Rural Assistance Committee) and Grameen Bank, are huge (with staffs of around 115,000 and 23,400 respectively) and were instigated, and are still directed, by single individuals. Both manifest a necessary degree of hierarchy at this scale, and utilize a "headquarters" and "field office" organization. BRAC, unsurprisingly at such a scale, is the largest NGO in the world, while Grameen is the home of the pioneering concept of microcredit, for which a Bangladeshi economist, and Grameen Bank's founder, Mohamed Yunus, won the Nobel Peace Prize in 2006.

One of BRAC's initial larger-scale successes was a campaign for oral rehydration—many children were dying from diarrhea, particularly in rural areas where there were not available medical care facilities for intravenous treatment. Fazle Hasan Abed, BRAC's founder, propagated an oral solution that had been shown to be viable, made simply from salt, sugar and water; the mission was purely educational— to teach rural women the recipe one by one. Although it took nearly ten years, the campaign was a success.

Grameen, on the other hand, refined a specific procedure, funding micro-scale, local business ventures. The organization still maintains the same requirement as when it was founded in 1976: five people organize, receive training, make initial deposits and slowly develop a usable fund.[11] Yunus' work on microcredit was to used maximize the potential of a small amount of resources—either that of a low-level donor, or that of the community itself—to produce discreet and accumulating results using other available social capitals as an accelerant.

Despite these innovations, or clear implementation and contextualization of innovations, what is most interesting is what happened afterwards. Abed thought that BRAC's success would be copied by other NGOs—he could simply test an idea, if it worked, it would catch on and other organizations, even institutions, aid agencies and the government would work cooperatively to magnify and replicate the test. When others didn't join BRAC's efforts quickly, BRAC decided to simply replicate itself; it would become its own consortium of NGOs. This gives the organization significantly more control over all aspects of its procedures, from testing, development, deployment to feedback—all form a closed loop, granted a very large closed loop. BRAC has had a Research and Evaluation Unit since 1975 to evaluate, and more importantly, refine its experiments.

Grameen decided to diversify, coming to resemble a multinational corporation, with the Grameen Family of Companies, in order to fund itself, rather than rely on donors. Today it is a network of companies and subsidiaries that handle everything from communications, to developing nutrient laden yogurts with Danone, Inc., to aqua and agriculture initiatives, to healthcare to for-profit enterprises selling Bangladeshi goods, all feeding back into the original banking nonprofit.[12] BRAC is similarly multidirectional, even including BRAC University, and both have expanded outside of Bangladesh, furthering the model of micro-work at macro-scales. While Grameen embeds the individual model in an identical totality, somewhat like a fractal, BRAC self-replicates to produce an impressive mass.

While growth seems to signal success (the larger the organization, the more people being helped) the question remains: how much quantitative progress has there really been? According to the international indices, Bangladesh is as poor as ever.[13] However, Grameen and BRAC are by all accounts successful, yet strangely, despite their mega-size, they are still not able to generate measurable change on a national scale.

Zones of governmental administration do remain— certain things that NGOs remain restricted from, such as control over zoning or land granting to building housing or reorganizing slums. Most slum dwellers in Dhaka are squatters—while slums occupy twenty percent of the city's area, ninety-seven percent of residents do not own their dwelling. Under current law, occupants cannot build until they own a land title, leading many NGOs to then address credit and lending, like BRAC and Grameen, which leaves housing to be provided informally until money can be saved to purchase land on which to build.[14] In this way, community-initiated and enacted development projects like ones that are found in Dharavi, Mumbai's largest slum, become impossible.[15] These moments clarify the limits of these giants' capabilities despite size, financial power and even promise and effectiveness. Their work begins at the micro-level and curiously for the time being, the effect seems to remain there; active on the local level. Despite the fact that NGOs might be adjacent to market-based practices, such as small for-profit enterprises (even in Grameen and BRAC's case of profit to fund a nonprofit), having diverse and fractured goals other than to make money seemingly renders results at a much slower and more nuanced pace than typical market returns.

Above: Yunus, in his office, won the Nobel Peace Prize in 2006 for his work on microcredit. Right: Grameen Bank's headquarters in Dhaka, Bangladesh.

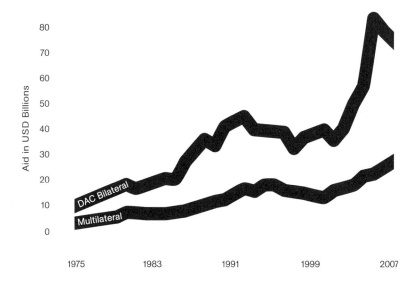

Bilateral aid flows reflect multiple political and economic histories and agendas. France, Portugal and the UK distribute a larger portion of aid to former colonies. In January 2007, the Venezuelan ambassador to Nicaragua described large and deliberate aid expenditures rather plainly: "We want to infect Latin America with our model."[4] Although former and neocolonial ties can be a major factor, it is rare that allocations of aid are perfectly synchronized with the donor's political motivations, let alone that the donor can cleanly control effects. Though a donor country may artificially guide aid flows to influence a desired outcome, aid is hardly a closed system of absolute or easily enforceable obligation.

Multilateral institutions, broadly concerned with economic development, are designed to be less directly subject to political influence than bilaterals. Member nations, as non-managing investors, are only allowed informal input at the yearly G8 or G20 summits. Of course, though, these investors choose the management, and among these investors, the most powerful nations are likely to have the most influence. Nevertheless, recipients are selected through mathematically rigorous assessments to determine which local environments might be most hospitable to development projects based on the economic and social values of the investor nations. The World Bank uses such assessments of countries to guide allocation of their low-interest loans; each year since 1997, they have calculated a country performance rating (ICP) that determines performance-based allocation. The World Bank's International Development Association (IDA) gives thirty-five to forty-year interest-free grants to seventy-eight IDA-eligible countries (for fiscal year 2009, eligibility is determined for a GNI per capita ceiling of 1,095 USD). This annual exercise in reviewing eligibility is undertaken by World Bank economists over a span of six months and is estimated to cost 1.5 USD million each year. Since its inception in 1960, the IDA has disbursed 193 USD billion with a recent average of ten USD billion a year. Half of total aid has been granted to Africa.

Part I: Country Policy and Institutional Assessment for the International Development Association (World Bank): First made public in 2000, and even then only in the form of aggregated rankings rather than detailed scores, the Country Policy and Institutional Assessment (CPIA) is the first part to calculating the ICP. The CPIA consists of sixteen indicators separated into four clusters, and each indicator is given a score between one and six. The most recent revision conducted in 2004 gives the following breakdown:

Economic Management: Macroeconomic Management, Fiscal Policy and Debt Policy

Policies for Social Inclusion/Equity: Gender Equality, Equity of Public Resource Use, Building Human Resources, Social Protection and Labor, Policies and Institutions for Environmental Sustainability

Public Sector Management and Institutions: Property Rights and Rule-Based Governance, Quality of Transparency, Accountability, and Corruption in the Public Sector

Structural Policies: Trade, Financial Sector and Business Regulatory Environment

Part II: Annual Report on Portfolio Performance and the Governance Factor for the International Development Association (World Bank):
In a simplified explanation, the resulting CPIA score is then given a weight of eighty percent. The other twenty percent consists of an Annual Report on Portfolio Performance rating (ARPP), which assesses each country's performance on implementing prior World Bank projects. Lastly, this weighted average of the CPIA and ARPP is multiplied by a governance factor, which is drawn from the governance-relate indicators above, effectively intensifying their impact in the ICP: changes in governance criteria have 6.07 times more impact on the overall ICP rating than do changes in non-governance criteria.

Multilaterals' institutional bias towards economic development has also led to harsh criticism in terms of doctrine ("priming states for global capitalism")[5] and met with uneven outcomes. Penalties associated with loan and grant conditions can be excessive for struggling borrowers. Conditions attached to the loans and grants perhaps come with the best of intentions, yet may not reflect the realities and capacities of borrower nations. Conditions may determine changes in borrower nation internal policy that may come into direct conflict with the interests of portions of that nation's population.

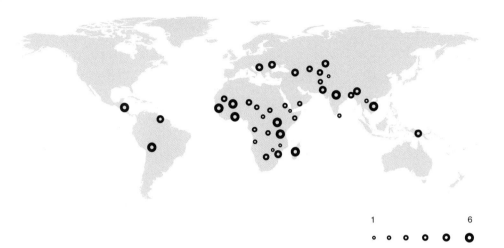

1   6

○ ○ ○ ○ ● ●

CAPACITIES

4

NGOs

NGOs, in contrast to both bilateral and multilateral organizations, tend to be more flexible in structure and are primarily accountable to their own prioritizations and criteria. Often, this involves the identification of inefficiencies or discrepancies in official aid flows and then working to fill the gaps in aid delivery. As a counterpoint to multilaterals' one-size-fits-all approach, NGOs' highly specific concentrations can be very effective for accomplishing a particular task such as focused disaster relief efforts. Unfortunately, this same characteristic can prevent them from seeing the larger picture surrounding the issue or problem that they aim to address.

Progressively, the three channels' coincidence has become the norm. Not only do missions overlap, but also membranes are becoming increasingly permeable to one another. For example, a significant share of ODA is distributed through NGOs, a policy initiative first implemented by the structural adjustment programs of the Reagan-Thatcher era. NGOs in particular have been much maligned for "selling out" by partnering with official sources of aid. Additionally, in taking on more capital and thus more responsibility, many NGOs have had to make drastic structural shifts, mimicking the very channels they hoped to balance. Such collaborations also bring to the surface challenges of accountability and transparency on both ends as each channel struggles to employ its full capability in a given situation without diminishing the effectiveness of the other.

NGO Personalities

	Service	Advocacy
Self	AARP 3HO Women's Savings Cooperative	RFSL Arab Women's Forum CIAA
Others	CARE Rotary WaterAid	Human Rights Defense Centre Mental Disability Advocacy Center

A sampling of NGO diversity:
3HO Foundation, Inc. (Happy, Healthy, Holy
   Organization, Inc.)
Academy for Future Science
Action Canada for Population and Development
Action Contre la Faim
Adventist Development and Relief Agency
Afghan Development Association
African Business Roundtable
Agency for Cooperation and Research in Development
   (ACORD)
Alliance Africa
All-Russian Society for the Deaf (ARSD)
Amazon System Information (SIAMAZ)
American Association of Retired People (AARP)
Amnesty International
Arab Women's Forum
Big Brothers Big Sisters International
Biopolitics International Organization

Care International
Caribbean Conservation Association
Caritas
Chernobyl Union International
Chilean Corporation for Children Youth Rights
China Arms Control and Disarmament Association
China Green Foundation
CIVICUS (World Alliance for Citizen Participation)
Confederation of the Food and Drink Industries of the
    EU (CIAA)
Co-operation Ireland
Environmental Development Action in the Third World
    (ENDA)
Ford Foundation
Fundación Alma
Global Water Partnership
Grassroots Ministries
Greenpeace
Helping Hands Worldwide
Human Rights Defense Centre
International Bodyguard Association
International Cultural Youth Exchange (ICYE)
International Federation of Women Lawyers
International Islamic Relief Organization
International Planned Parenthood Federation
International Society for Prosthetics and Orthotics
Italian Centre of Solidarity
Kimse Yok Mu
Madre, Inc.
Médecins Sans Frontières (MSF)/Doctors Without
    Borders
Mennonite Central Committee
Mental Disability Advocacy Center (MDAC)
Mercy Corps
Oxfam
Pacific Women's Watch (New Zealand)
ProChoix
Qatar Charitable Society
Rainforest Foundation
Relief International
Right To Play

Rotary International
Royal Society for the Protection of Birds
South Asia Partnership International
Special Olympics International
Stockholm Environment Institute
Sudan Association for Combating Landmines
Swedish Federation of Lesbian, Gay, Bisexual and
    Transgender Rights (RFSL)
Tearfund
The European Institute
The John D. and Catherine T. MacArthur Foundation
Transparency International
Turtle Island Restoration Network
Ukrainian World Congress
UNESCO Centre of Catalonia
Union of Arab Banks
WaterAid
Widows and Orphans Welfare Society of Kenya
World Muslim Congress
World Vision
World Wildlife Fund (WWF)
Young Women's Christian Association of Nigeria
Yugoslav Youth Association Against AIDS (Youth of
    JAZAS)

NGOs Rising

Beginning as informal, voluntary organizations, NGOs initially congealed into action around gaps in official capabilities from provision of local emergency relief to more systematic basic services.[16] Today NGOs occupy a range of positions in relation to governments and other institutions: from formal recognition to informal, from antagonistic relations to cooperative, from broadly focused missions to single-issue commitments. While this makes NGOs difficult to distinctly categorize as a group, on a practical level, the extraordinary diversity makes any comprehensive means of oversight or unfettered information sharing basically impossible. Despite what NGOs have collectively achieved, there has never been a formalized collective.[17]

If needs occur irrespective of political climate and ideology—and needs do—then so will NGOs. Former communist bloc countries did see a dramatic increase in NGO activity after the folding of the Soviet Union, yet this was part of an already ongoing wave of NGO influence and activity begun in the decades earlier. Lester Salamon marks the mid-1970s moment of final decline for the communist system, when recession won out over anemic growth, as a catalyst for NGO emergence in Eastern Europe.[18] This economic conclusion, long before the matching political one, necessitated supplemental systems to address needs unmet and services not provided by the government and generated numbers of organizations previous to the appearance of democratic institutions. In the 1980s, this was globally witnessed due to the public success of the Polish trade union Solidarity, from their declaration of their right to organize to the their subsequent leadership of the opposition in the first election in the Soviet Bloc.

Between 1990 and 1996, gross ODA disbursements to Sub-Saharan Africa fell by twenty-three percent as a result of a general loss of faith, coupled with internally restricted budgets.[19] In instances where populations were in need of assistance, but were governed by less-preferred recipients, donors increasingly looked for ways to give and distribute aid that circumvented government channels.

The importance of the initial structural similarities between the informality of the exploding communications sector and that of the exploding NGO sector in the 1980s has been suggested by Jessica T. Mathews. In her analysis, NGOs are a representation of the political and social instantiation of the telecommunications revolution, effectively dissolving the privilege of the state to be the sole collector and regulator of large quantities of information.[20] NGOs have taken advantage of new methods of communication, increased globalization and shifted attitudes about a global citizen's role and duty. In fact, these trends so strongly correlate that it is difficult to tell which combination functions as the scaffolding for the other's growth.

The unofficial nature of NGOs does prevent them from using formal channels for their own purposes, yet possible collaboration has never been categorically excluded. What today manifests as strong alliances directed towards a goal—some NGOs receive the majority of their funding from governmental sources and many institutions rely heavily on NGOs to carry out the implementation of their projects or provide insightful and informed guidance—began perhaps a mutually pragmatically beneficial situation. Both US President Ronald Reagan and UK Prime Minister Margaret Thatcher instigated policies to promote NGOs as a tactic to reduce social spending budgets.[21] At the same time, NGOs benefitted financially by formally registering with governments as nonprofit organizations. This concession of tax exemption has been the most prevalent means of governments' promotion of NGOs in the US, the Philippines, Japan, France, China and elsewhere.[22]

A tax credit alone, however, is not sufficient to run an organization; a steady influx of funding must be generated in order to begin, continue and grow. While twice as much NGO financial support comes from governmental sources as the private sector, a significant amount of funding, 4.7 billion by the mid 1980s, came from lateral private sources, such as foundations, charities and religious organizations. These larger organizations found local NGOs to be effective and directed vehicles of aid delivery.[23] This is particularly true of well-established western entities who looked to promote the emergence of these types of organizations in the developing world. Further, established private giving sources embodied and transferred a type of necessary "technical assistance," such as fundraising tactics, to developing organizations in addition to purely financial aid.

NGO proliferation has benefitted from multiple and concurrent forms of decentralization. As information collection, storage, retrieval and synthesis began to transform the previous model of a central archive, power structures began to transform also. Decentralization within larger entities allowed for more disparate sources of non-official participation and intervention, specifically information gathering, reporting and implementation, areas in which NGOs are credited with affecting significant improvements to the accuracy and effectiveness of the aid system. Entities such as the United Nations, World Bank and the OECD's DAC—themselves often operating in ways to bridge the fragmentation and multiplication of national entities—embraced and ushered NGOs into a variety of roles, from consultancies to partnerships to granting a participatory voice in decision-making.

The greatest public demonstration of NGOs' effectiveness occurred with the 1992 Earth Summit in Rio de Janeiro where 1,400 NGOs attended formally and 17,000 representatives enacted an alternative Global Forum. This event demonstrated the ability of NGOs to organize on a large scale as well as their capacity to come together in commitment to a singular issue of importance. The self-initiated NGO Global Forum was successful in creating an agenda and making clear policy recommendations that were later incorporated into the United Nations Framework Convention on Climate Change and the Kyoto Protocol, which has now been ratified and accepted by 186 countries.[24]

Since their first appearance, NGOs have become an increasingly institutionalized aid actor, which brings certain benefits, such as political leverage for their platforms, and certain negatives, such as redundancy with already-established institutions. What seems most notable from their emergence, and persists in large measure, is that—perhaps through competition, sheer fervor, or even pure numbers—the rise of the NGO as a "new"[25] entity has revitalized and brought greater optimism to the whole project of international giving.

> 1,000M USD

100M - 1,000M USD

20M - 100M USD

> 60,000M USD

20,000M - 60,000M USD

1,000M - 20,000M USD

1M - 1,000M USD

> 500M USD

100M - 500M USD

50M - 100M USD

20M - 50 M USD

1M - 20M USD

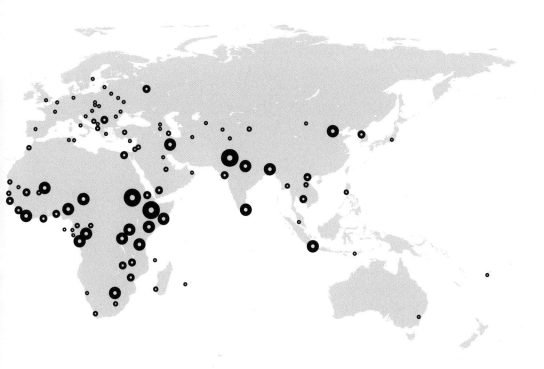

> 100,000 USD

50,000 - 100,000 USD

20,000 - 50,000 USD

10,000 - 20,000 USD

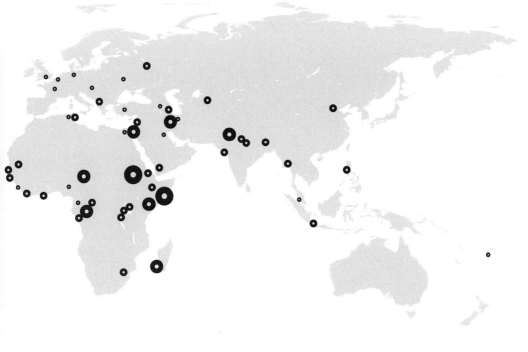

5
Challenges

Urgency and Proliferation

The issues that giving addresses rarely disappear. Inequity is a constantly moving and evasive target. The lone exception to this rule might be the global defeat of smallpox, certified as eradicated in 1979 by the World Health Organization. Such terminology migrated from the field of disease combat to the attitude one should take toward economic disparity overall. The concept of eradication—now commonly applied to addressing the effects of disparity—took on additional strength as the existing unequal distribution of resources grew to be seen as an unforgivable human rights violation.

Mandates calling for the immediate halt of poverty proliferated through aid channels, as well as calls for rigorous studies into inequity's component conditions. Poverty as akin to disease was thus firmly embedded in institutional rhetoric with the declaration of the United Nations' *International Year for the Eradication of Poverty in 1996*. Efforts to decrease inequity had previously been characterized as alleviation and then reduction; it was instead to be eradicated, once and for all. Poverty, formerly understood to be a fundamental fact of the human condition, was declared solvable and eradicable. Inequity was to be joined by an even more basic state, hunger, in the Millennium Development Goals laid out by the UN in 2000. While for the most part no one entity could be charged with causing economic imbalance, few could be said to be responding appropriately given the urgency of this potentially eradicable, solvable problem.

The complexity of the current global aid landscape signals that Aid Capital is responding to such a sense of criticality, one factor in its rapid growth. Aid Capital's increase is measurable through the expanding bounty of activity and flows that now rush forth to meet needs even during economic downturns. However, such complexity can counterproductively generate emergent bottlenecks, turbulence, unwanted outcomes, and cloudings of accountability. In this section, we look at several of the logistical challenges now faced by NGOs awash with attention and new opportunities. As well, we will see how national ideologies and personal agendas can manifest quite different tendencies in aid giving.

NGO Accountability and Cooperation

NGOs face external demands for greater organizational transparency, beyond statements of a given organization's aims and funding sources, to ensure ongoing proper internal monitoring of funding and resource distribution. While many large NGOs have established means of enforcing internal compliance, on the whole they remain much less transparent than either businesses or governments.

Cases of inner NGO strife have expanded the debate over their accountability to discussions of overall legitimacy and "representativeness" of their donor base.[1] Because NGOs produce much sought-after independent research and analysis, they are regularly called upon by government policymakers to evaluate important policy decisions. Critics, like activist and journalist Naomi Klein, have lashed out against calls to apply external regulations and oversight mechanisms to NGOs in the manner of corporations and governments, claiming that constraints will render NGOs ineffective.[2]

Though perhaps not as conspicuous to the global public as direct government involvement, NGOs—at least those which avoid official channels—have, through lack of perspective, risked aiding extremist regimes that use violence as a means of controlling its populace, as may have happened in the case of the perpetuation, or inadvertent support, of the Khmer Rouge along the Thai-Cambodia border during the 1980s.[3]

Managing Expectations: the American Red Cross

Regarded as the quintessential humanitarian organization, the American Red Cross is often stressed to its limits in times of disaster. Expected to step in to effectively manage any crisis, the American Red Cross faces challenges in efforts to expand support, alter organization, and prepare for the unexpected, no matter the magnitude of a crisis. Largely shouldering the burden of relief support in the absence of government attention to the aftermath of Hurricane Katrina in 2005, the Red Cross raised a remarkable two billion USD and mobilized 235,000 volunteers. However, the organization's prioritization of funding conflicted with donor expectations, leading to public anger when 200 million USD of donor gifts to Hurricane Katrina were revealed to have been earmarked to prepare for future crises rather than to supply assistance to victims of the disaster.

Responding to Criticism: The Nature Conservancy

Expansion and changes in management policy led to accusations in 2003 that the Nature Conservancy mission of "preserving biological diversity" had been severely compromised on its way to becoming the world's wealthiest ecological NGO.[18] Not only was the organization allowing for oil and gas exploration on some of its land holdings, it also was engaged in a kind of insider trading, selling prime conservancy land at reduced prices to supporters and trustees who agreed to certain development restrictions. The Nature Conservancy responded to the outcry, which came from as high as Capitol Hill, by promising to halt any drilling and to both carefully document and limit land sales to external donors only.

Lack of Coordination: HIV/AIDS-related NGOs

HIV/AIDS-related NGOs are a prime example of the way in which complexities are arise from having little transparency between similarly motivated groups. Their numbers and scope have exploded as a result of government subsidization and private giving, enabling them to provide much-needed treatment, prevention and education services. Yet their effectiveness is limited by their individual size and access to resources, a problem that could be resolved by a pooling of certain energies, but instead is perpetuated by an inability to effectively coordinate, let alone communicate, with one another. Ministers of Health in many poor countries "now express frustration over their inability to track the operations of foreign organizations operating on their soil, ensure those organizations are delivering services in sync with government policies and priorities and avoid duplication in resource-scarce areas."[19]

Competition for Funds: Rwanda

The proliferation of NGOs and private giving sources is often blamed for the accelerated fragmentation of the global aid landscape. Multiple organizations must compete with their peers for limited publicity. As soon as the 1994 Rwandan Genocide began to attract significant media attention, a huge influx of NGOs abruptly arrived on the scene. Andy Storey of Oxfam recalls that any given NGOs' failure to respond to the Rwandan crisis had the potential to discredit it with its donor base at home, even if the organization itself didn't see its intervention as either necessary or related to its self-defined aid role.[20] For many NGOs, having a presence in Rwanda was first and foremost a critical opportunity for public exposure.

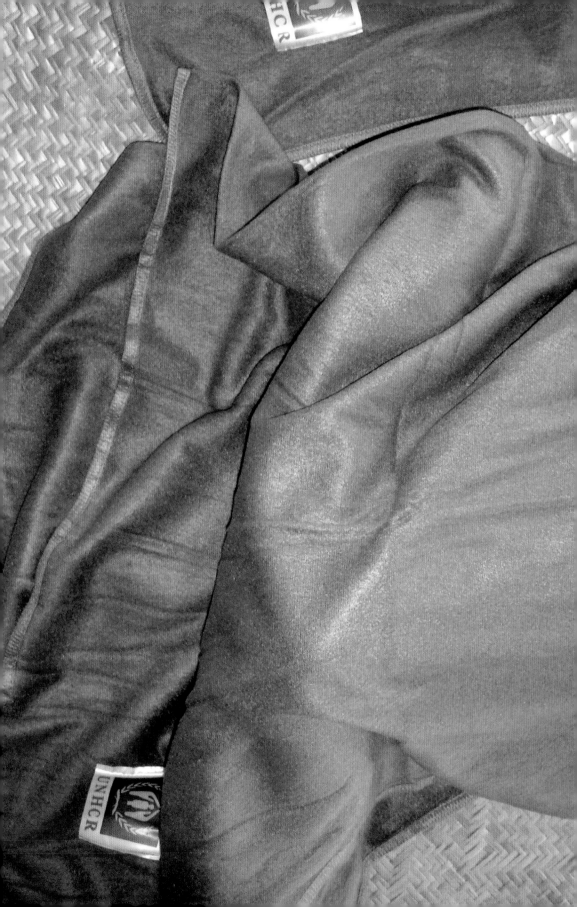

Diligence in Disaster Relief

On May 2 of 2008, Cyclone Nargis made landfall on the coast of Myanmar. An estimated ten billion USD in damage was incurred[4] and 146,000 lives were lost.[5] As aid began to trickle in slowly from international aid organizations and NGOs, the local Junta initially refused most shipments on the grounds that they would not grant visas for the aid workers waiting to distribute them. On May 6, 2008, four days after the initial impact of Cyclone Nargis and amidst international outcry, the Myanmese representative to the United Nations finally made an official appeal for aid.[6]

By May 9, a DHL (Deutsche Post DHL) Disaster Response Team (DRT)–a ten to fifteen person volunteer group composed of employees at the German logistics giant—had gone to work and the UN World Food Program (WFP) had made its first shipment to the region in the form of thirty tons of emergency relief equipment including stretchers, generators and water purifiers. The DHL Disaster Response Teams program is a partnership with the United Nations Office for the Coordination of Humanitarian Affairs to provide airport logistics support to crisis areas in the aftermath of a sudden-onset disaster such as the cyclone. DHL DRTs operate out of region-specific bases in Miami, Dubai and Singapore, in a network of coverage that serves ninety percent of the world's at-risk regions.[7] Since the program's inception in 2003, DHL has already responded to a number of such natural catastrophes, including Hurricane Katrina, the Indian Ocean Tsunami in Sri Lanka, Cyclone Nargis in Myanmar and earthquakes in Iran, Peru, and Indonesia.[8]

The importance of distribution and logistics is well known in the aid community. Even when material resources are readily available for aid, the management of these resources determines whether or not they actually reach their intended recipients. The flow of aid materials can be so great in the aftermath of a disaster that infrastructure is often pushed beyond capacity and the system breaks down. After the 2003 earthquake in Bam, Iran, it took only four days for the airport to become so inundated with unsorted aid materials that it was forced to block all incoming shipments for weeks.[9]

The partnership of DHL with the UN represents the degree to which diligence—the simple care and thought given to the task at hand—can have a tremendous effect on the successful delivery of aid. In its commercial operations, DHL invests a great deal of time and money into the development of technological solutions to logistics. While automation and digitization techniques are the focus of much effort in innovation, the work of a DRT is, by contrast, remarkably low-tech. The tools DHL brings to the job are simple: work clothing, necessary information and communication technology such as cell phones, pallet trolleys, office supplies and start-up operational supplies.

Twenty-five minutes southwest of Yangon airport in Myanmar, the DHL DRT set up in a 3,050 square meter warehouse leased from a local rice exporter by the UN. DHL was charged in the following weeks with organizing the flow of aid from international charter aircraft, through the airport and on to local distribution centers dispersed throughout the disaster region. After restoring power and setting up communications with the building, now the UN Common Warehouse, the DRT organized local workers to staff the floor and established a system to organize and palletize the flow of relief materials. By the time of their departure in June, DHL staff had trained locals in the basics of air freight and warehousing, who were then able to take over the operations for a more manageable flow of aid.[10]

The DHL DRTs conscientiously work to relieve the crisis sight unseen in the generic condition of a warehouse. Purposefully making the airport warehouse their sole domain, distribution is left to state, military or private actors with local knowledge and familiarity with the political terrain.

A UNHCR (United Nations Refugee Agency) standard-issue blanket.

Governmental organizations like the UN Humanitarian Relief Depot will repair roads and infrastructure leading away from the airport in order to facilitate the flow of aid and will often handle transportation of aid materials into the disaster zone. The key is being able to calmly and intelligently receive, sort, inventory and pass on parcels of international relief materials. Only on the final day of each mission is a trip taken to the disaster area itself, providing a sense of accomplishment and completion for the DHL volunteers. DHL's focus is micro, in contrast to the UN's macro focus.

The question of why the United Nations is not able to do this on its own is a worthy one. Why should a multi-lateral organization with billions of dollars at its disposal and equally significant amount of responsibility not be able to handle a task as routine and basic as the management of a warehouse floor? The UN does, after all, have an entire division that should be dedicated to this task: the UN Humanitarian Relief Depot (UNHRD) based out of Brindisi, Italy with hubs on four continents. Moreover, why should it resort to partnership with a private-sector organization for such a thing? Does this not constitute a conflict of interests or opportunity for undue influence?

Diligence has been a very difficult thing for the UN to come by. With the best of intentions the UN has repeatedly found itself under-funded, understaffed and overtaxed with new and expanding responsibilities. Between 1988 and 1993, thirteen new peacekeeping operations were launched, as many as during the previous four decades.[11] An August 1994 headline in the *New York Times* cited understaffing as a major hurdle in UN efforts to monitor human rights in Rwanda, with only three of a total twenty planned monitors showing up, lacking communications equipment or vehicles to allow them to move around the country.[12] OECD funding to the UN has been declining since the 1960s[13] and the core UN budget, funded by a regular system of mandatory assessments from member states, is notoriously difficult to maintain—member states have repeatedly refused to pay for political and financial reasons. Most famously, throughout the 1990's the United States Congress refused to authorize payment of UN dues as a means of protesting the amount that the US government was asked to pay. In 2008, Japan, Germany, China, Argentina, Iran and Greece ran arrears of the Regular Budget ranging from 11 to 210 million USD each.[14] When added to the US's outstanding 846 million USD, this accounts for a total of 1.13 billion USD in funds unpaid to the UN. In such a complex and difficult financial and political climate, the UN was forced into a more large-scale managerial role that relies on outside organizations' varied resources to supplement its efforts. For better or for worse, the UN began an active campaign to court the funding and resources of business under former UN Secretary-General Kofi Annan.

Still, the pragmatic observation can be made that the private sector has developed knowledge and technological innovation that the UN has simply not had the time or money to develop itself. This is perhaps the context within which the DHL partnership was made with the United Nations. Isabelle de Muyser-Boucher of the UN Office for the Coordination of Humanitarian Affairs puts it very simply: "DHL allows us to draw on expertise that we cannot afford to maintain all year long."[15] This statement speaks to an argument that given the general movement towards privatization in the politico-economic climate, these kinds of partnerships should be inevitable.

Yet, others hold that it is the UN's role as a governmental institution to remain independent—that partnerships with businesses deny the UN an autonomous role as critic and thus these relationships constitute a conflict of interests. Indeed, the UN does seem to have followed this trajectory. The United Nations Center on Transnational Corporations, itself founded in the 1980s as a pioneering organization to mitigate the undue and inevitable influence of global businesses and to empower developing nations against their abuses, now focuses on the positive effects of transnational corporations, and the ways in which developing countries might attract their Foreign Direct Investment.[16]

Critics cite this general shift in tone as one that has permeated the UN on all levels. Secretary-General Ban-Ki Moon now makes an almost philosophical claim that the interests of business and government are inseparable—that the work of the United Nations can be viewed as seeking to create a more ideal, stable environment within which business can thrive.[17] The apparent success of DHL's partnership with the UN shows otherwise. It is instead the careful and conscientious work of effective volunteers that creates a more ideal, stable environment within which the UN can thrive.

DHL's Disaster Response Team manages the supplies coming to the warehouse in Myanmar.

Above: Supplies are distributed by UN workers to the areas struck by the cyclone.
Below: The blankets were handed out to victims of 2008's Cyclone Nargis in Myanmar by the UNHCR.

Bilateral and Multilateral Risks

While NGOs may face difficulties due to their diverse structures and discrete identities, bilateral and multilateral foreign aid channels can cause trouble in recipient nations due to the built-in imbalances of power. Such lack of parity has both the capacity to elicit "soft power" demands for reciprocity, as well as overstepping attempts to direct aid once it has crossed international borders. Opinions vary among donors regarding the benefits of supplying aid to an economy via the government (centralized) or through NGOs and other grass-roots mechanisms on the ground (decentralized).

Enabling "Rogue States" through Aid

One accusation levied at foreign aid is that the donation of large sums of money through official, or government, channels allows leaders out of favor with the international community to maintain power within their boundaries. Arguments against the central distribution of aid cite a history of governments who have either been unsuccessful at creating policies which reach development targets or have used aid money to maintain purportedly uncivil practices, such as increasing personal wealth or, most catastrophically, to fund civil war and acts of genocide.[21]

In contrast, arguments supporting the central distribution of aid make the point that this model provides for greater accountability between donor and recipient countries, as well as between the citizens and authorities of the recipient country. Some contend that supporting local governance can help to build citizen trust and confidence in the capabilities of local authorities.[22] However, many critics disagree with this strategy, citing that if a government's primary source of revenue comes from foreign aid—extreme cases being Ethiopia and Gambia whose budgets consist of ninety-seven percent aid subsidies—it has less reason to be accountable to its citizens than to its foreign investors.[23]

Imposing Penalties

One early reason identified for the inefficacy of bilateral foreign aid was the problem of perverse incentivization. The dominant aid paradigm after World War II focused on—in rather simple terms—flowing money into poor countries as a means to jumpstart economic growth. Many recipient governments, however, kept economic and political conditions constant. Aid flows thus remained constant, serving to maintain rather than "improve" the economic status quo.

In order to ensure than money given as aid would be spent in a manner stipulated by the donor, structural adjustment programs were adopted in the late seventies and early eighties by donor countries and multilateral institutions alike. The programs imposed various conditions on foreign grants, loans and debt interest rates in an effort to reduce budget disparities at the receiving end. Failure to meet the conditions would normally be reprimanded with fiscal penalties and trade barriers.

The measures were meant to be disciplinary, yet the penalties incurred could severely hamper real development. For instance, as recently as 2004, the United States collected almost as much money in import duties on Bangladeshi goods (314 million USD) as on French imports (350 million USD), despite buying Bangladeshi products amounting to only 1/14 the value of those from France. This is because the taxes levied on Bangladesh were much more stringent than those on France, enforced as a consequence of accused governmental corruption. However, Bangladesh is by all classifications a poor, agriculture-based economy that needs to import many raw materials and goods to enable its domestic manufacturing sector. Through the imposition of higher taxes, the US policies reduce spending within Bangladesh, ultimately hindering internal economic growth.

Despite the fact that structural adjustment-type restrictions can make aid a real challenge for recipients, there are mechanisms built in the official aid system to alleviate such conditions. Debt reorganization, also known as "restructuring," is used by bilateral and multi-lateral institutions to offset penalties. If the repayment of a loan is preventing money from being allocated to development, then the donor or creditor can alter the terms of the loan to extend its repayment period, or forgive the loan, extinguishing it altogether.

Tied Aid

Bilateral donor governments can ultimately stunt growth in the economies they seek to assist through the tying of aid, requiring that funds must be spent only on goods and services offered by the donor country. Donors may overstep and try to keep a too-tight grip on how and where funding is spent, or may simply provide purchased goods and services in the most costly manner. As a result of tying aid to specific commodities and services and not subjecting them to normal market forces, development project costs can increase by as much as thirty percent.[24]

Tied and Food Aid as Percentage of Country's ODA (2007)
Source: OECD

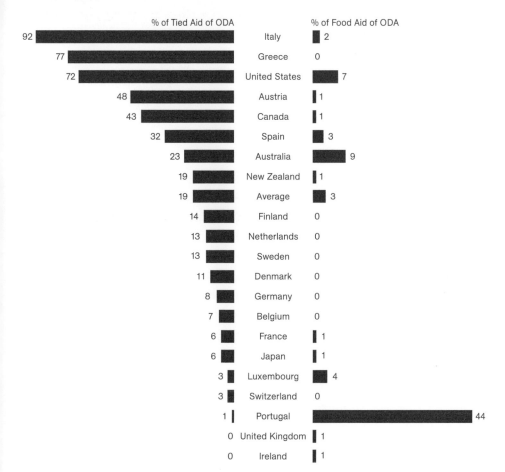

% of Tied Aid of ODA		% of Food Aid of ODA
92	Italy	2
77	Greece	0
72	United States	7
48	Austria	1
43	Canada	1
32	Spain	3
23	Australia	9
19	New Zealand	1
19	Average	3
14	Finland	0
13	Netherlands	0
13	Sweden	0
11	Denmark	0
8	Germany	0
7	Belgium	0
6	France	1
6	Japan	1
3	Luxembourg	4
3	Switzerland	0
1	Portugal	44
0	United Kingdom	1
0	Ireland	1

The OECD report *The Tying of Aid* (2006) found that the motivations for tying aid were both economic and political. Although most donor countries give aid to a wide variety of recipients, they clearly attached value to individual recipients with which they have, or hope to have, strong relationships and the intent to exert or maintain influence to some degree. From an economic point of view, the donor country might also tie aid as a way to artificially stimulate its own exports. The study found that exports related to tied aid constituted about four percent of a donor's total exports; while a seemingly low figure, four percent, could amount to a significant amount for a large nation, tipping a trade deficit into a surplus. In 2001, in an attempt to untie aid, the donor members of the DAC agreed to aim to untie virtually all aid to the Least Developed Countries.

Food Aid

Food aid can also hinder a recipient economy, albeit in slightly different ways than tied aid. Food aid is aimed at providing food and nutritionally related assistance to tackle hunger in emergency situations, as well as in more sustained long-term hunger alleviation efforts. Often criticized for dumping excess agricultural production on low-income markets, food aid is regarded as one of the most ineffective forms of aid. Not only does it have an extremely high cost of delivery (in the US, cost of transportation represents as much as sixty-five percent of total expenditure of food aid),[25] but this form of aid also suffers from donors' inadequate coordination, poor response time, and the reality that food could almost always be purchased more cheaply locally.

Ideologies of Giving

Japan
Despite ten years of economic stagnation and a budget deficit, Japan is still the second biggest ODA donor after the US. Tying only 6 percent of total aid and providing very little food aid, Japan has recently taken steps to gain international goodwill by shifting from donor-beneficial economic infrastructure aid to increasingly social-infrastructure-oriented aid.

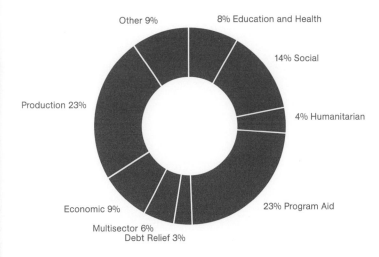

Other 9%
8% Education and Health
14% Social
4% Humanitarian
Production 23%
23% Program Aid
Economic 9%
Multisector 6%
Debt Relief 3%

United States
As the biggest donor of ODA, the US still ranks in the midfield in terms of aid standards. Not only is 72 percent of all US aid tied, but the majority of its foreign aid flows to areas of recent military intervention. These numbers are indicative of how the complexities of foreign policy, military and media affect aid decision-making in times of crises.

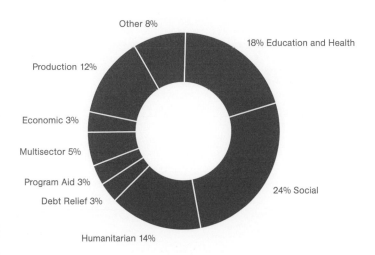

Other 8%
18% Education and Health
Production 12%
Economic 3%
Multisector 5%
Program Aid 3%
24% Social
Debt Relief 3%
Humanitarian 14%

Norway

Norway is at the forefront of recipient-sensitive international development. Not only does it have impressively low overhead costs but it also
does not tie any aid or provide food aid. Despite the global financial
crisis, Norway is projecting to give 1 percent of its total GNI in 2009 to
ODA, while DAC recommends that member countries aim to allocate only 0.7
percent of GNI.

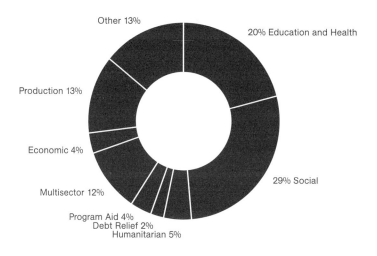

Other 13%
20% Education and Health
Production 13%
Economic 4%
Multisector 12%
29% Social
Program Aid 4%
Debt Relief 2%
Humanitarian 5%

Portugal

Of all DAC donors, Portugal allocates the most significant portion of its
aid to former colonies, among them Timor-Leste, Angola, Mozambique and
Guinea-Bissau. Additionally, food aid accounts for 4 percent of Portugal's
total official aid, also the highest among DAC donors.

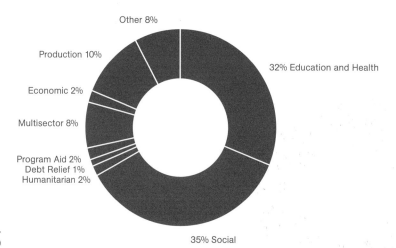

Other 8%
Production 10%
32% Education and Health
Economic 2%
Multisector 8%
Program Aid 2%
Debt Relief 1%
Humanitarian 2%
35% Social

Sponsored Identities

Bangladesh

Classified as a least-developed country, Bangladesh received the majority of its aid in 2007 from the UK and received almost as much DAC donor aid as it did multilateral aid. However, Bangladesh's GNI increased only 34.4 percent from 2003 to 2007, compared to the average GNI increase of 84 percent for all OECD developing countries.

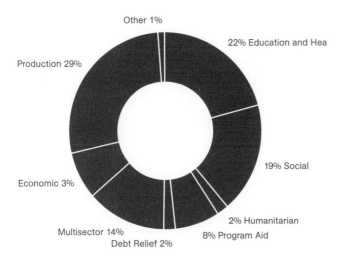

Other 1%

22% Education and Hea

Production 29%

19% Social

Economic 3%

2% Humanitarian

Multisector 14%

8% Program Aid

Debt Relief 2%

Sudan

Sudan received by far most ODA from the US (710 million USD versus the second-most from the UK at 206 million USD) and received over five times more from DAC donor countries than from multilaterals. As a least-developed country, Sudan has seen an increase of 154 percent in GNI from 2003 to 2007.

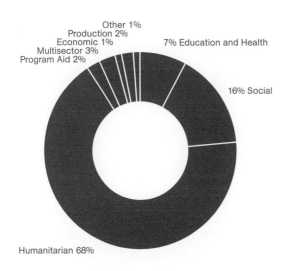

Other 1%
Production 2%
Economic 1%
Multisector 3%
Program Aid 2%

7% Education and Health

16% Social

Humanitarian 68%

China

Having received the majority of its ODA from Japan, China receives over four times more from DAC donors than from multilaterals. A low-middle income country as categorized by the OECD, China has seen a 10 percent increase in GNI from 2003 to 2007.

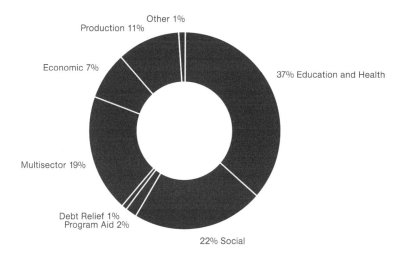

Other 1%
Production 11%
Economic 7%
37% Education and Health
Multisector 19%
Debt Relief 1%
Program Aid 2%
22% Social

Nigeria

While receiving the greatest amount of its ODA from the Netherlands—with Austria as its second biggest donor—Nigeria receives twice as much from DAC donors as from multilaterals. Nigeria, a low-income country, has experienced an impressive 163 percent increase in GNI from 2003 to 2007.

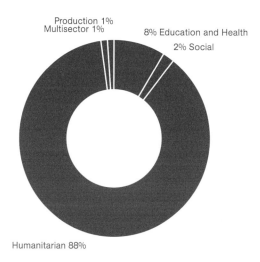

Production 1%
Multisector 1%
8% Education and Health
2% Social
Humanitarian 88%

NGOs, despite being independent entities, can play politically coercive roles as well. To an extent, their activist roots inherently make them political and ideological by nature. Yet, their growing dependence on ODA grants for funding makes them susceptible to the political agendas of a supportive government. This is evidenced by the fact that both Swiss and Japanese NGOs tend to echo their governments' preferences for working with countries that vote in tandem with their own objectives in the UN.[26] In some donor countries, NGOs are responsible for distributing as much as twenty percent of ODA.

Sometimes motivations tend to be more didactic than overtly political—as in the case of multilateral institutions, which offer their aid conditionally, and paired with advice. Though they lie outside the range of specific political biases, they have received criticism for promoting or imposing a unitary vision of growth and development, with specific economic system implications. However, as Nobel Prize-winning economist Joseph Stiglitz acknowledges, "Multilateral aid is often more effective than national assistance, because it is not so closely linked with the agenda of any particular country; that makes the aid more effective and the advice more readily accepted."[27]

Private Aid

The problem of translation between a donor and recipient country may be self-evident at a state level, but this relationship is mirrored at the individual donor level. As ODA and multilateral channels are closed to them, private donors must either give through NGOs or develop their own organizations. It would deny the soft power of government to say that this private giving is not at all influenced by the economic or political climate. Yet, increasingly, individual giver and mega-giver agendas are becoming a dominant force in giving. Such influences are unavoidable, though possible to minimize, in situations of giving. Potential givers have the capacity to be mindful of giving's inherent complexity of motivations and the diverse ways in which Aid Capital may increase. First-time donors are likely to donate again, in larger amounts, encouraging others to follow their example. Private donations, along with all the other forms of giving discussed in this book, while never infallible, have always generated more Aid Capital.

Breakdown of Private Giving (US 2007)
Source: Giving USA 2007

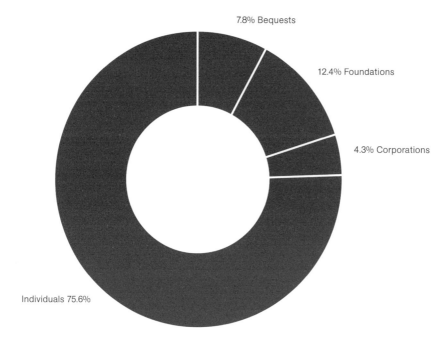

7.8% Bequests

12.4% Foundations

4.3% Corporations

Individuals 75.6%

Cultures of Giving

Even though international giving is traditionally seen as a task of the government, in nations where private philanthropy is encouraged, private givers may even contribute a larger amount of funding to international human development efforts than the state itself. Variations in state and private giving tend to reflect the varying social priorities of governments and their citizens. Countries where government responsibility extends to public services typically have limited philanthropic economies, while more market-driven nations assume that the responsibility lies with those in the private sector.

    The most direct form of incentivization is tax structure, which tends to reflect official attitudes toward private charitable activity. Countries with tax policies that offer incentives for individual giving and a wide-reaching policy of tax-exemption often have reduced social welfare allocations and larger philanthropic economies. Promoters of laissez-faire practices tend to offer tax breaks for donations, allowing private citizens to decide where to allocate their money for social benefit. These policies allow the worthiness of causes to be determined by individuals rather than countries, arguably favoring eccentric values over collective needs.

Impact of Economic Climate on Cultures of Giving

	Free Market	Government/Non-profit Partnerships
Examples	United States	Austria, Belgium, Netherlands
Overview	Countries that promote a free market model of philanthropy leave it to their citizens to decide where their money is best spent, foregoing tax revenues in favor of individual choice. The US government gives relatively little money to social programs, and even less to the arts and culture, leaving gaps that are filled in by the philanthropic sector.	In government/non-profit partnerships, the state funds the non-profit sector and provides for basic needs, with little reliance on private philanthropy. Citizens willingly pay higher taxes, which the government uses to support independent non-profits, such as arts and cultural organizations.

		Free Market	Government/Non-profit Partnerships
History	Tradition	Individual autonomy and limited government role	No tradition of charitable giving
	Economic Impact	Economic boom increased amounts of private giving and the formation of new grant-making foundations	Not applicable
Characteristics	Civil society	Civil society sector comprised of paid and volunteer workers	Large civil society sector, comprised of paid employees
	Volunteer Component	Small	Small
Role of State	Civil Society	"Hands-off"	Partnership between state and non-profit sector
Taxation for Charitable Giving		Tax deduction	Small tax deduction
Funding		Individual and corporate gifts to private foundations	Tax revenues to public and non-profit sector
Allocation of Giving		Religion, higher education, arts, culture	Education, culture, arts, basic social and human services
Reliance on Private Charitable Giving		Significant reliance	Limited reliance on private philanthropy
Advantages		Compensates for gaps in government budget Assumed social responsibility Individual choice of cause	Ensures basic services are provided Promotes redistribution of wealth
Disadvantages		History of corruption Does not promote redistribution of wealth Tendency for donations to go towards cultural causes rather than basic needs	High taxes Shifts responsibility from individual to thestate

	Post-Communist	
elfare States		
nland, Norway, Sweden	China	Russia
elfare states embrace policies that ovide publicly funded and administered cial services and cultural programs, sulting in limited use for private ilanthropy and non-profit sector. tizens willingly pay higher taxes and ust the government to provide for the llective good through state-run social ograms.	Welfare states embrace policies that provide publicly funded and administered social services and cultural programs, resulting in limited use for private philanthropy and non-profit sector. Citizens willingly pay higher taxes and trust the government to provide for the collective good through state-run social programs.	In Russia, corporate donations from domestic companies and multinationals, along with donations from wealthy oligarchs, provide a large proportion of charitable funding, 90% of which goes to state-run bodies. In January 2006, President Putin signed into law a measure to severely limit the activities of NGOs.
o tradition of charitable giving	Family and social groups tend to take precedence over the broader community	Tradition of pre-revolutionary charity confined to the aristocracy
ot applicable	Current transition from a centrally planned economy to a market economy	Current transition from a centrally planned economy to a market economy
rge civil society sector, comprised edominantly of volunteers	Emerging civil society	Emerging civil society
rge	Large	Small
ands-on"	State administered	State administered
o tax deduction	Tax deduction Provision in the tax code permits some deductions for direct donations to state institutions	No tax deduction Viewed by many as poorly administered
x revenues to public sector	Largest source of nonprofit finance from government funding	Largest source of funding from corporations to public and nonprofit sector
ducation, culture, arts, basic social and uman services	Health care, education, poverty alleviation	Health care, education, poverty alleviation, and to foster democratic ideas, principles, and institutions
mited reliance on private philanthropy d nonprofit sector	Significant reliance to improve socioeconomic conditions and strengthen civil society	Significant reliance to improve socioeconomic conditions and strengthening civil society
nsures basic services are provided omotes redistribution of wealth	Compensates for gaps in government budget Centralized managment of funds	Compensates for gaps in government budget Assumed social responsibility
gh taxes nifts responsibility from individual to e state	History of corruption Shifts responsibility from individual to the state	History of corruption

US Federal Budget 2007
2.77 Trillion USD

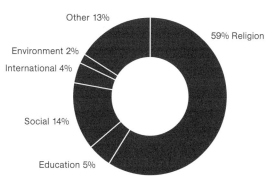

Other 14%
3% Education
Environment 1%
Foreign Aid 1%
Debt 9%
Military 19%
55% Social

US Individual Donations 2007
295.02 Billion USD

Other 13%
59% Religion
Environment 2%
International 4%
Social 14%
Education 5%

Canadian Federal Budget 2007
222.21 Billion USD

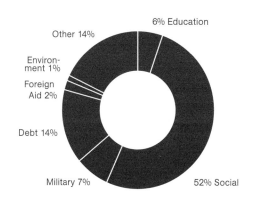

Other 14%
6% Education
Environment 1%
Foreign Aid 2%
Debt 14%
Military 7%
52% Social

Canadian Individual Donations 2007
9.98 Billion USD

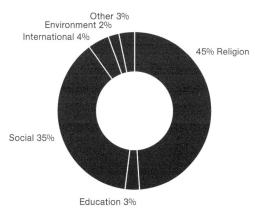

Other 3%
Environment 2%
International 4%
45% Religion
Social 35%
Education 3%

Swiss Federal Budget 2007
55.34 Billion USD

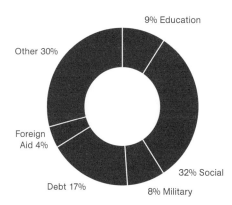

9% Education
Other 30%
Foreign Aid 4%
Debt 17%
32% Social
8% Military

Swiss Individual Donations 2007
1.1 Billion USD

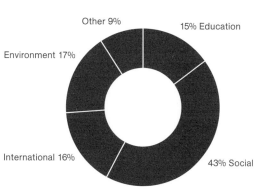

Other 9%
15% Education
Environment 17%
International 16%
43% Social

The Individual Giver:
As a form of control, giving can be seen as the actualizing of one's motivations to implement a desired outcome. In this sense, giving empowers both states and individuals to move privately held beliefs into the public sphere. Today, the majority of private donations —international and domestic—comes from individuals and is therefore tied to a variety of priorities and personal interests. Unlike governments, who should at least assess need when budgeting, individuals are under no such impetus. As a result, they are free to give according to individual perceptions, intentions, desire and of course, self-interest.

The Mega-Gift:
The growth of philanthropy worldwide reflects larger shifts in social policies. In the past decade, social class disparity has increased in most developed countries. At the same time, the last decade has seen great increases in the number of very large donations from private sources. In the US, the number of one hundred million USD-per-year gifts has risen from two in 1996 to twenty-five in 2007. Mega-gifts allow recipient organizations to grow quickly by providing funding for new programs and building projects. They also draw great public attention, which can lead to an influx of subsequent donations. Individuals (and governments) often trust that an organization must be worthy if a mega-giver is prepared to bestow their mega-gift upon an organization. In that sense, mega-gifts can represent the ultimate form of control related to giving, where a single donor holds the power to influence state-scale contributions.

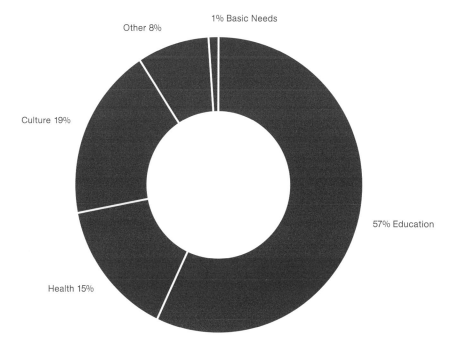

Lifetime mega-gifts have become a critical source of funding due to the decreasing rate of personal bequests, once considered a staple of high-end philanthropy. This trend is revealing of the increasing importance of having life-long control over one's donations, particularly in terms of its benefits to the philanthropist's public image. Whereas a bequest usually confers some control over the donation to the donor's remaining family post-mortem, the mega-gift concentrates power in one person's hands and emphasizes an individualistic life-long approach to wealth and power.

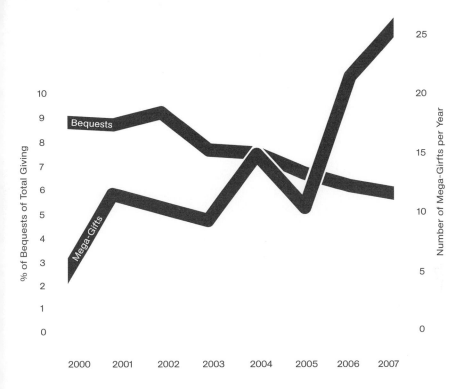

Giving presents an opportunity to reconcile and synthesize two seemingly opposite values: that of individualism and that of the common good. A donation is an expression and reinforcement of individual beliefs and values, but one that is ultimately meant to benefit the collective. The question of control becomes important when the common good is to be defined—wholly or in part—by the giver. Individuals, institutions and governments all use mechanisms of aid as tools to exert control, whether it is over the outcomes generated by their gifts or the public perception of themselves as givers or honorable recipients. For those who have the means, philanthropy can also become a powerful mechanism for reinvention. Through acts of giving, one can diminish the public's memory of prior (or ongoing) misdeeds by appearing generous, kind or community-minded. Giving also establishes a public relationship between the giver and recipient, inextricably linking reputation and image.

Dependency States

Many argue that the provision of aid can produce dependency of recipients upon donors, but both parties can perpetuate this reliance. On the donor end, critics argue that aid is used primarily as a power-leveraging medium rather than the stimulator of development that it claims to be. Demba Moussa Dembele, the director of the Forum for African Alternatives argues that, in this way, "aid is an instrument, not a gift."[28] From the recipient perspective, corrupt regimes may purposefully sustain their state's economic condition to ensure the continual flow of aid funding. Though structural adjustment programs and similar mechanisms have been implemented to relieve this problem, they also tend to further incapacitate growth, also ensuring the necessity of continual aid provision. These relationships are not only unstable due to sudden changes in foreign aid policies, but also because they diminish empowerment and accountability between local citizens and state when the state does not occupy a provisory role.

Many aid critics strongly believe that allowing free market forces to stimulate development is the best remaining alternative. Perhaps most notably of late, Dambisa Moyo, formerly of the World Bank and Goldman Sachs, argued that: "aid undermines the ability of Africans, whatever their station, to determine their own best economic and political policies."[29] African economist James Shikwati, Moyo and others favor micro-financing and direct investment strategies, which have proven successful in certain situations. In a study conducted by the OECD, the amount of private investment going to Africa had begun to outpace aid. However, citizens don't necessarily see real, tangible benefits because foreign direct investment (FDI) tends to capitalize on tourism and the extraction of resources rather than infrastructural development. There have even been perverse environmental effects as a result of FDI, as evidenced by the heavy presence of foreign oil firms in Nigeria,[30] whose investors unanimously disapproved of recent calls to overhaul and regulate the country's oil and gas industry.[31]

Perhaps the greatest challenge to direct investment—as revealed in a period of recession—is its own dependency on the global market. Foreign investors are forced to react swiftly to shifts in global prosperity by canceling funding or involvement. Such is the case in Rwanda, where the holding company Dubai World recently pulled out the majority of a 230 million USD investment in the Rwandan tourism sector. The investment had been hailed as a boon for the Rwandan economy, which now must seek other means to accommodate shortfalls and debt and new means of investment. Whether aid flows are in the hands of central governments or individuals, they rarely lack in underlying motives, be they economic or political. The more integrative aid channels become—in addition to swelling in size and scope—the more difficult they are to track and ensure. At the same time, their overall integration and capacity, when well managed, contin-ues to strengthen and grow. Aid Capital gladly propa-gates itself when given opportunity.

6
Exchange

Structure of Capitals

All relations of exchange, giving or otherwise, are mediated by a structure of capital, where capital is defined as a particular quantity's capacity to render effects outside of itself.

"Particular quantity" can designate anything—a person's muscle-power, the crop-capacity of a field, a tool's capacity to reduce exertion, etc. Having no inherent value in itself, capital is a value system, or more precisely, a system of value systems, which cycles through periodic phases of accumulation and expenditure; the former translating external forces into abstraction, the latter reversing this process in an effectual application of the reserve. This translation of capital is the predominant vehicle of power in its movement across social, political and cultural boundaries. In order to reconcile the values of its ubiquitous participants, capital has developed a bifold technique of abstraction and differentiation to track its mutations.

The abstract, numerical form of financial (or "economic") capital requires little transformation to transact quickly and flexibly, and despite its relative newness is perhaps the most immediately recognizable form of capital. As a result, finance dominates most all discussions of social dynamics—to the extent of veiling and marginalizing capital's more nuanced forms.

In fact, within the framework of capital, various facets can be identified, each with its own degree of uniqueness and communicative overlap with the others. Of these, it is useful to make a general distinction between the quantitative and qualitative forms, adopting sociologist Pierre Bourdieu's framework of "economic" and "symbolic" capitals.[1] Alone in the former category is the aforementioned financial capital. Among the latter group, one finds human capital, political capital, social capital and cultural capital.[2] Human capital is a measure of the value of an individual's faculties and capacity for labor and productivity. Political capital describes the value of an individual's influence in a larger social field, placing emphasis on the persuasive power of qualities like prestige, influence and public image. Social capital evaluates the synergetic advantages of collaboration, agreement, shared resources in interpersonal or group relations. Finally, cultural capital—a more general concept itself comprised of multiple variations—establishes the value of the individual relative to institutional formalizations of authenticity and credibility.

These various forms of symbolic capital are not linked by a universal exchange rate. However, as capital, lacking any value without implementation or translation outside of themselves, it is impossible to evaluate any one without consideration of its equivalences with and distinctions from the other(s). Essentially, no form of capital can exist in isolation, nor can it work its influence without conflict and consequence. The ultimate finitude of material resources can bring about a competitive prioritization of the individual over the social. In this case, capitalist value systems become a mechanism for accumulating and defending localized concentrations of power, against and at the expense of others. This logic problematizes acts of giving, which often become obscured or confused by moving against financial capital's prevailing values of ever-increasing concentrations of quantifiable assets.

Considered only within the framework of financial valuations of capital, giving can only be patronizing and oppressive, reducible to pure optimizations, or a serious error in judgment on the part of the giver. There are, however, forces of capital that work against the discrepancies inherent to the capitalist desire to create imbalance—namely, that of Aid Capital.

Aid Capital would prefer not to exist—in the sense that it works against the system of imbalance that necessitates its existence. Aid Capital is a beneficent antagonism inherent to the dynamics of capital itself, which would otherwise tend toward unmoving reserves paradoxically evacuated of any value. Aid Capital renews value. It looks to short circuit the feedback loop that focuses capital into ever-tighter circles. It appropriates the various powers constitutive of other capitals to apply them to the production of external effects, expanding its own capacities beyond itself. This refusal of consolidation generates a double benefit, flowing toward both the recipient and the giver.

The primary asset of Aid Capital—what will move it forward in its proliferation—is the increasing capacity for communication that allows expressions of need to reach those capable of response. Each time this occurs, it is matched by further mobilization of good will and inspiration. Aid Capital, in this way, invites all other capital to abandon the exclusive economies of scarcity and enter an intentional, participatory and affirming economy of plenitude.

Flows of Aid Capital

Channels of aid have distinct strengths and weaknesses. Each channel can improve, becoming more efficient while remaining fully accountable, becoming more precise while remaining inclusive, or becoming more flexible while not becoming rash. Each could collect larger amounts to give but remain resilient to the forces of corruption, as well as demonstrate timely results while remaining patient. Altogether, the problems of aid channels represent a field of competing/cooperating entities and their attempts to translate intentions into desired outcomes.

Further, the mutability of the gift itself, a condition particular to Aid Capital, is only marginally under the control of the gift's global agents, guards, conveyors, transformers and actors. A gift of foreign aid undergoes a series of phase shifts en route from donor to recipient, rendering any prescriptive or restrictive process ineffective. The end result will always be something of an unknown. Even in the most seemingly simple situation of immediate need, any gift is fundamentally projective—with the ultimately desired effect abstracted from the materiality of its object.

For example, consider a scenario in which individuals give a small sum of money to help build a school in a developing country. The money is collected by one of these individuals or a chosen organization and then transferred to a bank in the target country. Here its value will be translated into raw materials and conveyed further as payment for the temporary labor of construction. This represents a shift from Currency A, to Currency B, to discreet raw materials and labor (with a residual transfer of Currency B to the providing business and the temporary workers). An architect, engineer and workers then cohere these materials and labor into the form of a building. This building further provides *the capacity* for jobs for some teachers, possibly attracts further funding for books and school fees, and ultimately, an education for children.

If, however, the educational agenda became detached from the financial value of gift along the way, passing from hand to hand, organization to agency to government to NGO, the gift might turn into anything, something even counter to the giver's agenda of education. Perhaps a building may be built, but not a school. In order for Aid Capital to flow back to the giver and accrue to the receiver, some element of the donors' original intent needs to remain intact throughout the transformative procedure. As well, the particular aspects of the recipient's need must help shape the donors' original intent. Third, the aid must remain agile enough to adapt to emergent circumstances.

Alternatively, a similar scenario, a housing project, shows how lack of clear communication of need and maintenance of intent might be of some benefit, but not the one expected. In this instance, a multilateral bank wishes to build new housing units as part of a development aid initiative that includes upgrading available habitation. Donor countries' contributions to the bank, plus capital earned in the market, are applied to the project. The bank's capital becomes currency, utilized to purchase raw materials and labor in the project country. The material purchases resonate as business for local suppliers and employment opportunities arise due to the labor required. Materials are assembled and transformed into cohesive units, ready to be occupied.

And yet, these units never become actual homes. Improvements in shelter can provide stability for families, be a long-term market asset and provide sanitation infrastructure, which can positively impact health. In this example, however, the designated occupants instead remove all valuable fixtures such as piping from the new housing units and sell them. Rapidly, and not through a real-estate transaction, the gift is converted back to currency. The currency is then used to buy food, medicine and other basic provisions, all of which have the potential to provide a tangible and short-term stability, and in the case of medicine, may have a lasting impact on health.

A third scenario: an organization provides food aid to a country that is in the midst of turmoil. The government is not stable and is perpetuating a disruption of normative activities and operations such that the citizens no longer have access to the basic necessities for survival. Under these chaotic conditions, food and water are provided intact by a humanitarian organization and shipped directly to the afflicted country. The supplies must initially pass through the hands of those in power. The hegemonic group then transforms the relief into currency by selling it to the initial intended recipients instead of distributing it as free aid. The currency is then used to purchase weapons to ensure the ruling group retains further power.

This instance seems to support measures like tied aid, suggesting that it is perhaps better to restrict a gift as a preventative measure against its misuse. However, such a "pure" gift's impotence, or lack of resilience, is both a clearly quantifiable loss in terms of expense and a less quantifiable loss in terms of opportunity and reach. Aid Capital has the potential to be generated at each site of transformation. Materials or supplies purchased in a donor country and transported internationally can be exponentially more costly than if acquired locally. More importantly however, is that by the time materials are actually purchased, decisions have already been made that may limit the project's flexibility, and thus its—and the gift's—ability to capitalize on unforeseen possibilities.

Of course, none of this is a guarantee, which is precisely why each stage of a gift's phase change, translation or transformation is crucial to its overall definition. Ideally, in order to maximize the generation of Aid Capital, there must be some sort of trained supervision present at sites of transaction, holding joint allegiance both to the giver and the recipient. This someone or something must contain the expertise, authority and cultural know-how to witness and supervise the exchange in order to maximize the flow of Aid Capital's complex surpluses toward the recipient, toward the giver and laterally toward the others involved along the way. At the moment of each shift, the gift has renewed potential, even at the termination of a simple transfer of a "unit" to a recipient. Will they like it? Or want it? Do they hate it? The question arises: is something still a gift if it is not wanted, or is despised?

Architecture Aid

As aid agencies must dutifully pursue their agenda of helping and giving, the role of design disciplines is to articulate the desire to help (expressed as varying policies) and the help itself (much more constant—such as housing or infrastructure) simultaneously. Even though planners and architects may be influenced by trends and theory from other disciplines, they also function as concrete translators combining the values of their field with the contemporary desires of social and economic policy. Frequently collaborating as *consultants*, they are charged with strategizing and marshalling the process of giving through its initial phase of materialization by a client, namely the donor, aid or development organization, or a donor government. In this situation, they are given the task of providing projects with a useful design and capability for further expansion. They must further design replicable procedures, should one prove successful.

Doxiadis' Influence: Project Sites

Turner's Influence: Project Sites

Each collaborative project functions in some part as research for the next, with all parties, but primarily the donor, interested in how to improve the process. For the recipient, a particular project's success is important, while the aid agency may need to be content with how lessons learned will feedback into subsequent projects. Architects and planners, however, have the added capacity, above concern for a particular project or aid as a general project, to then feed their new knowledge into their discipline, essentially reframing aid's results as something that can inform practices beyond the unique conditions in which they were born. While an architect or planner would certainly be concerned about how a project performed, it is arguable that even if the production of a desired result was shared by the entire team, disciplinary or personal criteria could lay elsewhere.

Catherine Bauer Wurster + United Nations

Catherine Bauer Wurster, a self-proclaimed "Houser," was sought out by the United Nations for her relentless dedication to improving low-income housing and ability to influence public policy. Wurster graduated from Vassar College with an English degree in 1926 after a short stint in Cornell's architecture program. She became a leading housing activist and public advocate in the 1930s and 40s. In 1934, she published *Modern Housing,* in which she applied the successes of European housing to her vision for the US. This publication, along with her influence as the executive secretary of the Regional Planning Association of America, confirmed her authority in the field. In 1946, Wurster proposed the formation of the UN Housing, Town and Country Planning section, initiating her association with the UN, which would continue to contract her to travel, write and advise on housing matters in developing countries. In 1954, she organized a major exhibit on housing in New Delhi under the auspices of the UN HTCP. In 1958, the Ford Foundation employed her to design a master plan for Calcutta and later for Delhi.

In 1960, President Eisenhower appointed her to discuss the urban environment in *Goals For Americans* with the Commission on National Goals. Wurster's work for the UN has served as fuel for optimism in subsequent UN housing initiatives.[3]

Jacob L. Crane + United Nations

Jacob Leslie Crane received a degree in civil engineering from the University of Michigan and a planning degree from Harvard in 1921, where he studied under John Nolen. As a housing advocate in the United States, Crane initiated the idea of aided self-help, originally as an extension of resources beyond urban areas, specifically in the rural south. Crane recognized that families in developing countries are rich in human capital, and argued to provide tools, rather than products, to harness their potential. Although self-help schemes were considered failures in the US, they garnered attention abroad, and Crane's expertise was sought after internationally. He worked as a housing consultant in over twenty-five countries, for both government agencies and the UN. In Puerto Rico, he served as consultant to government agencies and industrial development companies, where he provided advice on public housing, low-cost private housing and cooperative housing, as well as the financing of mortgages. As consultant to the UN Department of Social Affairs and UN Housing and Planning and Technical Assistance Administration, and as chairman of the UN Mission to southeast Asia on tropical housing, he produced the earliest UN reports of self-help which would inform the 1964 *UN Manual for Self-Help* twelve years later.[4]

Michel Ecochard + United Nations, Moroccan Government

French archeologist, architect and urban planner Michel Ecochard was employed as a regional development planner, and as a consultant, he focused on solving problems of rural-urban migration. Ecochard studied architecture at the *École des Beaux-Arts* in Paris in the late 1920s. He began his career working on a city plan for Syria from 1932 to 1942. As the director of the Morocco Department of Urban Planning, Ecochard, together with Vladimir Bodiansky, experimented with housing design from 1946 to 1952, influencing an emerging generation of architects, most notably his fellow members of *Congrès International d'Architecture Moderne* (CIAM). Ecochard and *ATBAT-Afrique*, (the African section of the research center and atelier, *Atelier des Bâtisseurs*) developed an urban planning technique utilizing an eight-by-eight grid based on a traditional Moroccan development for Casablanca, intended to replace slum neighborhoods. In 1953, he received a consultancy position for the UN to design refugee housing in Karachi, Pakistan. His approach to Karachi's problems was similar his work in Casablanca. He felt the refugee problem was an indicator of larger issues of aggressive densification and proposed an evolving framework for the settlement of refugees, prescribing increasing levels of density coupled with increasing modernization. Individual units were designed to meet CIAM's four functions: dwelling, work, transportation, and recreation. Instead, the scarcity of resources dictated a piecemeal implementation and it was clear that finished housing was impossible to provide. This would prove to be the first sign of ineffectiveness of exhaustive planning in the developing world. Local resistance to his proposal brought on a general resistance to opacity in the national government and the UN, and would effectually factor in to the UN's decisions about partnerships in the future. As Ecochard's mission with the UN was ending, he accepted a commission with Pakistan's government to design the Karachi University campus. This proved to be a minor scandal, putting into question the opportunism and careerism of the UN's experts.[5]

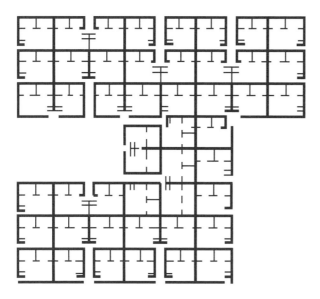

Otto Koenigsberger + United Nations

Architect, planner and Egyptologist Otto Koenigsberger's pursuit of a body of knowledge of building in tropical climates brought additional foresight to self-help policies. As a student of Hans Poelzig and Bruno Taut at the Technical University, Berlin, Koenigsberger learned the value of practicality and social responsibility. His experience as Chief Architect and Planner of Mysore State, India from 1939 to 1941, and Director of Housing and Ministry of Health for the Government of India from 1948 to 1951, exposed him to the dissonance between western building practices and their applications in developing countries. In 1951, challenging the assumption of the importance of universalism in modern architecture, he established the Department of Tropical Architecture at the Architectural Association in London, in order to understand the physical conditions of tropical countries. It was there that he and his students published the *Manual of Tropical Housing and Building.* From 1954 to 1981, Koenigsberger served as the chief UN Planning and Housing Advisor, beginning with a joint mission with

Charles Abrams to the Ghana. In 1957, they were sent to Pakistan to propose self-help schemes unlike any tried previously, in which they provided only essential core construction and services, allowing for immediate occupation and transformation of the site. Following his experience in Karachi, Koenigsberger published many articles on "action planning," rejecting the conventional "master plan" as unsuitable for the developing world due to its universal projection of slow, traceable growth and homogeneous culture. Instead, Koenigsberger's action planning preached dynamically adaptable plans that harmonized with the changing circumstances of a locale. In 1963, his position with the UN sent him to Singapore, where he attempted to implement action planning with Charles Abrams and Susumu Kobe. In 1973, the Ford Foundation called on his expertise, for which he produced *Infrastructure Problems of the Cities of Developing Countries*.[18]

Charles Abrams + United Nations

Charles Abrams, recognized principally for his contributions to social housing policy in the US, especially with regard to issues of race, was also one of the UN's most valued experts in the fifties and sixties. Obtaining a degree by attending night classes at the Brooklyn Law School, forming his own partnered practice, then investing in Greenwich Village real estate, Abrams acquired a political savvy and humanitarian agenda that not only helped him found the New York City Housing Authority but later gave him great insight in solving issues in the developing world. From 1947 to 1949, Abrams cultivated his direct style of communication as the *New York Post's* housing columnist. Abrams set about his missions for the UN analyzing an existing condition and answering with what he called a "gimmick" to stimulate social action. This strategy emerged during his second mission with the UN and Otto Koenigsberger in Ghana in 1954, where Abrams recognized personal home-savings accounts in cumulative, backyard stockpiles of weathered building materials. Diagnosing these as frozen assets, Abrams advanced a building and savings program, coinciding with a roof-loan scheme by which the government gave standardized loans for the elements of a home which people were unable to create themselves: roofs, windows, and doors. With this program, the government was able to stimulate local building of houses, which would locate Abrams' ideas within the realm of self-help. The program was extremely successful, provoking unanticipated social results such as the formation of community groups under the guise of "roof-loan societies," sharing knowledge and devising plans for their future. In some cases, Abrams' program proved to be almost too successful, as corrugated metal roofs began to be seen as achievable status symbols even in areas where indigenous thatched roofs were the better solution for the local climate conditions. Abrams would later adapt similar roof-loan strategies to Bolivia and Nigeria, but continued to innovate in the context of established local order in Kenya, Pakistan, India, the Philippines, Ireland, Japan, Jamaica and Singapore with the UN, as well as in Calcutta and Chile with the Ford Foundation.[19]

Constantinos Doxiadis + Ford Foundation

The Ford Foundation's partnership with Constantinos Doxiadis was initiated to foster the development and realization of the architect's theories. Doxiadis' Ekistics is a science of human settlements, freed from political or cultural realms by its elementalism. Doxiadis studied architecture and engineering at the Technical University of Athens and the Berlin Charlottenburg University, receiving a PhD in 1936. He served as a Chief Town Planning Officer for the Greek Army during World War II, and was afterwards involved in Greece's reconstruction. He opened his own firm in 1951, quickly launching development projects in over forty different countries. He became intensely involved with the Ford Foundation, receiving over a period of two decades the largest personal award to date, allowing for a proliferation of exposure to Ekistics in developing countries in the Middle East and Asia. In 1954, he was involved in a mission for the International Bank for Reconstruction and Development (IBRD) in Syria and Jordan. In 1955, Jacob Crane convinced the Development Board of Iraq to commission Doxiadis for the National Housing Plan for Iraq, for which he proposed new housing and community facilities in existing cities, and even new villages for industrial workers in desert areas, effectively synthesizing his involvement with the Middle East. Doxiadis' work in developing nations, although secured by the promise of Ekistics, often resembled the work of his contemporaries as he advocated for aided self-help and core-construction programs. Doxiadis was nothing if not determined, theorizing on urban development until his last day, even as he suffered with Lou Gehrig's disease.[20]

Evolution of Dynamic Ekistic Systems, Constantinos Doxiadis

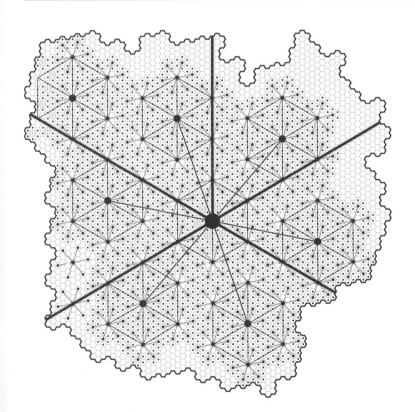

Building Human Capital

Since its conception in 1976 by Millard and Linda Fuller, Habitat for Humanity International has built and rehabilitated 300,000 low-income homes for 1.5 million people worldwide.[6] Habitat's guiding principle, drawn from the Old Testament states, "If a brother living near you becomes poor, you must provide for him…do not make a profit on the goods you sell him." Just as it is said that a monetary currency un-tethered to a gold standard floats on faith in government, it is certain that a volunteer currency floats on faith in the organization. While "faith" seems a precarious business plan, it is perhaps an aid agency's greatest asset.

In addition to coordinating financing, materials and volunteers, Habitat gives direction and operating principles that support more than 2,250 affiliates internationally. Former US President Jimmy Carter has been a vocal proponent since 1984, raising funds, volunteering to arrange and construct houses on "building blitzes" and establishing the Rosalynn and Jimmy Carter Work Project.[7] In 1996 US President Bill Clinton awarded founder Millard Fuller the Presidential Medal of Freedom, calling Habitat for Humanity "…the most successful continuous community service project in the history of the United States."[8]

This recognition comes despite the organization's non-profit nature, which necessarily limits the availability of monetary and material resources to accomplish its projects. Despite this scarcity, Habitat has identified a paradoxical abundance of human capital. A simultaneous condition of abundance and scarcity has particular resonance today. The digital age is often characterized by increasing amounts of free information existing alongside increasingly scarce material resources and many industries are currently negotiating methods of incorporating free information into the existing market framework. Despite sharing similar basic assumptions about human nature, what differentiates Habitat's notion of abundance from an informational model is its ability use monetary deficiencies to its benefit. [9]

Financial deficit allows Habitat to position human capital as the foundation of an operational model oriented toward sustainability rather than a commercial paradigm of either efficiency or quantity of product and profit. Goodwill, a stimulant of human capital, must be maintained, and benevolence towards Habitat's agenda, projects and the organization itself is produced in part by the lack of monetary resources. Rather than accumulating profit, Habitat carefully feeds its more limited financial resources into future projects. In addition to "sweat equity"–the working hours a receiving family must contribute–beneficiaries contribute a down payment and commit to a monthly mortgage.[10] The returns on these mortgages are not absorbed by the organization, but are instead placed into a rotating fund that sponsors future construction. While the greater budget of a commercial venture could objectively produce more, and perhaps better, housing, this would ultimately erode the desire to give to Habitat in the first place.

It is paramount that Habitat for Humanity continually cultivates human capital as its most valuable resource. The volunteers' commitment to and investment in the project and organization is developed through the process of building a house. A team of volunteers is comprised of around fifteen people—typically a diverse group of Americans—and is headed by a team leader with Habitat experience. Once an affiliate office has identified recipient families, Habitat's Headquarters organizes a trip, for example to a village in Ghana. After landing in Ghana, the team will travel from Accra to the chosen site where they consult with the village chiefs and local mayors—who are often western-educated with degrees in fields such as agriculture, economics or architecture—to determine parcel locations and site layout for the homes. For several weeks, volunteers work alongside the partner

Nzoku, a homeowner from the 2007 Habitat for Humanity Desmond Tutu Build, inside her family's Habitat home in the township of Mfuleni, near Cape Town.

families, with some contractor oversight, laying bricks and mortar, installing windows and roofs until the basic three-to-four room home is completed.

In addition to airfare, volunteers pay for room, board, transportation and other associated costs along the way—including a donation to the host-community's building program.[11] If Habitat's purpose is to build houses, it can be argued that there are better ways to allocate the 3,000 to 4,000 USD dispensed by each volunteer for a few weeks of simple physical labor. As a practical strategy however, Habitat has identified the surplus value of volunteers' personal involvement with the afflicted, and as such their costs may be a price worth paying over that of a more disconnected means of aid.

The onsite engagement of the volunteers is mirrored by the responsibility of the recipients. Critics frequently deride Habitat's insistence that families meet financial criteria, charging that by insisting partner families carry long-term mortgages, Habitat occludes the poorest from access to the program.[12] In North Carolina for example, a minimum income of between 20,125 USD and 38,500 USD was required in 2004, despite the government-established poverty level being 19,500 USD. This put an upper-range Habitat recipient at a higher income than forty percent of US families. Yet, Habitat's lending practices and insistence on "sweat equity" provide the family with a stake in the process and ensure that they will be able to maintain the house and a mortgage.[13] In this way, the human capital of committed beneficiaries contributes to projects that are defined by long-term success, rather than immediate alleviation. The careful choice of recipients may not include those who need houses most, but it produces a stable product that reflects well on the organization and those it helps, which in turn contributes to the longevity of its operations.

Adaptability is equally important to organizational persistence—a willingness to respond to change in order to remain stable. Habitat is flexible in its use of materials and strategic in their deployment, integrating local modifications based on climate, culture and availability of resources, after early mistakes using western construction methods and materials in foreign environments.[14] In order to streamline legal procedures and material procurement, in-country affiliates use qualitative criteria determined by Headquarters—rather than a universally imposed physical form —to develop plans. The plans conform to local codes and conditions, which can then be adjusted on a family-by-family basis. When concrete block is unavailable, as in many parts of Africa, local masons will be contracted to fabricate earthen bricks onsite. Earthquake-prone Sri Lanka uses steel-reinforced concrete block, where flood-prone Papua New Guinea requires the construction of the house to be raised on timber stilts to keep the occupants dry.

Habitat also avoids being stubborn about type. While the organization most often builds with single-family domestic use in mind, it recognizes that a simple building can house multiple families, or be used as a storehouse or a small business.[15] In comparison to prior architectural theories assuming a rigid correlation between a building form and its intended function, this can be considered a rather progressive understanding of the relationship between plan and use. Further, Habitat devotes resources to address lacking infrastructure and access to utilities. In partnership with local governments, they have built wells, set up power-lines, improved roads, purpose-built schools and multi-unit dwellings in villages where housing was being implemented. The organization has also adapted its financial practices, switching to microfinance and flexible lending arrangements to extend its reach into urban and semi-urban areas.[16]

Habitat's flexibility has even extended to a complete reversal of its mission-implementation strategy. With the foreclosures and subsequent population withdrawal that accompanied the decline of the US auto industry in Michigan in 2009, Habitat began demolition activities.[17] The organization entered into an agreement with the local government to demolish two derelict, vacant houses a week for two years. Additionally, Habitat is engaging more intensively in the rehabilitation of US foreclosed homes in lieu of new construction.

Habitat alone will never eradicate substandard housing, and thus, its criteria for success differs from that of a business—it will probably never achieve what it sets out to do. Instead, its prioritization must be organizational longevity, to continually address a constant need. In a not-for-profit economy, it can access other motivations for action than simple self-interest, providing the necessary abundance of human capital for the infinite task at hand.

Mfuleni, is approximately forty kilometers east of Cape Town in South Africa. It began to grow in the late 1990s; many of the housing structures are tin and are still not connected to utilities.

Seven friends from Horsham, UK went to South Africa to participate in the build, along with 120 others. The 2008 Tutu build was a partnership between Habitat for Humanity UK and Habitat for Humanity South Africa. Twenty houses were completed in the one week project.

Hassan Fathy + United Nations, Aga Khan Foundation

Hassan Fathy consulted the United Nations in matters of housing, as well as town and regional planning, emphasizing the importance and intelligence of vernacular forms. He promoted an appreciation for local, traditional building techniques imbedded with centuries of climatic design solutions, efficient building techniques, and social values and psychological preferences. Fathy was trained as an architect in Egypt, graduating in 1926. He began his career working at the Department of Municipal affairs in Cairo, then teaching at the Faculty of Fine arts. In 1945, he was delegated to design and supervise the New Gourna Village at Luxor, to displace the inhabitants of the Old Gourna from the Antiquities Zone, whose livelihood was robbing and selling treasures from the Pharaonic tombs. Fathy's model village was designed with abstract interpretations of traditional Egyptian typologies, drawing from a variety of provinces from Cairo to Nubian villages. His references appeared in the form of building material (brick mud), structural articulation and respect of the values of Islam. However, New Gourna Village's construction was interrupted after three years of planning and building, and the villagers refused to move in. Fathy placed the blame on an uncomprehending society, despite intractable interchange differences between villagers and authorities. The failure of New Gourna would eventually give rise to skepticism of the possibility of authenticity and sensitivity in architects co-opting vernacular in broad strokes. Despite New Gourna, Fathy's strategy was still recognized internationally as exemplary, and from 1950 to 1953, he served as consultant to the United Nations Refugee World Assistance program. In 1957, Doxiadis asked him to join his team as a housing consultant, giving Fathy an opportunity to pilot his strategies in Iraq and Pakistan. Doxiadis' scientific rationality illuminated for Fathy that in order for his ideas to translate to the broader context of regional development discussions, he would have to harness his fascination with craftsmanship, detail and tectonics to design reproducible types. Fathy then returned to Egypt in 1961, starting his own practice dedicated to his interest in local solutions. In 1963, he published what would become *Architecture for the Poor*, in which he occasionally employed the logic of Doxiadis to justify his philosophy. This same year, he was assigned to the United Nations Organization for Rural Development Project in Saudi Arabia.[22]

Research: Personal Study of Egypt's Vernacular Building Technologies, Materials and Spirituality Adapted to the Specific Needs of Old Gourna Villagers.

GIVER TAKER

A New Village: New Gourna is Built to Displace the Inhabitants of Old Gourna, but They Refuse to Move in.

GIVER TAKER

Christopher Alexander + Various Governments

Christopher Alexander consults as an expert on the form of environments and their effect on human civilization, which positions him as an asset to the full gamut of planning undertakings. Bridging computer science and architecture, he argues that a city is a complex organism with an underlying order and works to find an exactitude in the built world—a recognizable, digestible network of patterns. His *Pattern Language* is a guide to the science of design, or a "generative grammar," democratic in that it equips anyone to build successful environments. Alexander studied architecture and mathematics at Cambridge, and completed a PhD in architecture at Harvard. He founded the Center for Environmental Structure in 1967 and is a professor in the Department of Architecture at the University of

California, Berkeley. He has worked as a consultant to city, county and national governments, and has advised corporations, government agencies, and architects and planners globally. One of his most notable projects is an experiment in low-cost housing in Mexicali, Mexico, sponsored by the Governor of Baja California in 1975. Rather than design the houses, Alexander and his students designed a generative construction code for the community to build their own dwellings, resulting in a complex of semi-unique structures, unified by their adherence to Alexander's philosophy. Only five of the thirty initially projected houses were built, due to a new national government's discontinuance of funding. Eventually, inhabitants built walls and fences corresponding to lot lines in municipal documents, defining their individual properties, thereby eradicating the public space formed by the cluster arrangement prescribed by Alexander. This initial gesture of subdivision snowballed into a complete deterioration of Alexander's pattern, until the Mexicali project bore no resemblance to its original intent, as it coalesced with the surrounding structures in material, tectonic and even interior arrangement.[22]

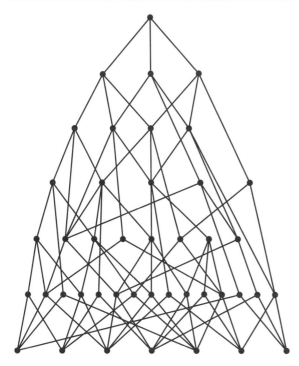

N. John Habraken + SAR (Foundation for Architects Research)

Habraken served as the Director of SAR (Foundation for Architects Research) in the Netherlands from 1965 to 1975, where he investigated methods of adaptable housing. In *Supports, an Alternative to Mass Housing* published in 1962, he proposes a distinction of *support* from *infill* in multi-unit dwelling, in order to exploit the economy of standardization without sacrificing diversity and character of individual contribution. Habraken was born in Bandung, Indonesia and graduated as an architect from TU Delft in the Netherlands in 1955. He had a long teaching career, both at Eindhoven Technical University and MIT, from which he retired in 1989 after serving as the head of the Architecture Department from 1975 to 1981. Habraken was instrumental to the discourse of social housing at the time, insofar as Open Building applied the principles of self-help development schemes to the scale of a single structure of mass housing. Unlike Christopher Alexander, Habraken's desire for participation was not a question of democracy, but rather diversity: a critique of the institutional quality of mass housing and its failure to speak to a society. Habraken was interested in defining a new role of housing authorities: to support, rather than shape society. His most recent book, *Palladio's Children*, is an examination of the architect's unchanging mirror image through a history of transformations in the architect's actual role.[23]

Liu Thai Ker + Singapore Housing and Development Board

Architect and planner Liu Thai Ker is known for public housing and development planning in Singapore. Holding prime positions with the city's planning department, Thai Ker formed a uniquely integrated relationship with Singapore, synchronizing his initiatives with those of the city authorities. He focused on optimized solutions for housing a growing population, while maintaining undeveloped space and reducing congestion. Thai Ker studied architecture at the University of South Wales and MIT, then worked for I.M. Pei and Loder & Dunphy in New York. Upon returning to Singapore, he helped the government come closer to their "Home Ownership for All" policy, completing over half a million dwelling units during his tenure with the Singapore Housing and Development Board (HDB) from 1969 to 1989. His largest contribution in shaping Singapore was shifting the public housing concept from large-scale estates with localized facilities to new towns consisting of high-rise towers with high plot ratios but low floor area ratios, which for Thai Ker was the only practical option for meeting the demands of the population within the horizontal restrictions of an island. Following a period of major reconstruction, Singapore was criticized for being too clinical in feel. In response, as CEO and Chief Planner of Singapore's new Urban Redevelopment Authority beginning in 1989, Thai Ker revised the Singapore Concept Plan to concern itself with national identity and heritage conservation. His unabating commitment to reducing automobile traffic in collaboration with the power of Singapore's strong central government later prompted the UNDP and UN-Habitat to seek his assistance as a consultant on matters of transportation.[24]

Charles Correa + "New Bombay" Development

Indian architect, urban planner and theoretician Charles Correa has worked to amalgamate modernism and non-western vernacular, not only in aesthetic and function, but also process, often infusing his concept with potential for incremental growth. Climate is his fundamental form-giver, with density and access as the best indicators of a city's health. After studying architecture at the University of Michigan and later MIT, he established a private practice in Mumbai in 1958. Dissatisfied with the municipal master plan of 1964, Correa published an alternative that elicited enough attention for the government of Maharashta to adopt it, acquire additional land, and establish the City and Industrial Development Corporation (CIDCO) with Correa positioned as chief architect. His alternative plan proposed the creation of Navi Mumbai, located across the bay from the then current urban density. This new quasi-urban growth center would provide for two million people, ideally with a density able to support both a light transportation system and an agricultural economy simultaneously. Correa's proposal for Navi Mumbai reconciled climatic conditions with financial limitations, exploiting what he called "open-to-sky spaces" as trade-offs against the cost of roof enclosures. Few of Correa's intentions for Navi Mumbai were realized. The most robust manifestation of his principles was Belapur, an artist sector of Navi Mumbai consisting of low-rise, high-density, freestanding cluster housing arranged to form a repeated hierarchy of public space. In this mixed-income site, Correa distributed land equally and according to the needs of the highest standard and designed the houses with the simplest structure, in order to give individuals the incentive to improve incrementally. When Belapur was completed in 1985, Correa was appointed by the Prime Minister as the first Chairman of the National Commission on Urbanism. Twenty years later, one third of the houses at Belapur were demolished and replaced, one third significantly altered and expanded, and one third remaining as originally built. Although this may indicate success of Correa's project as stimulus, the original village's appearance of equity and community has been lost, and the economic variety within the development exacerbated; the least affluent reside in the original dilapidated structures, and the most affluent have congregated into exclusive clusters and maximized their sites with larger, updated houses. Belapur is nevertheless still regarded as a unique, diverse, and intimate area. Currently the Farwell Bemis Professor at MIT's Department of Architecture, Correa continues to present the village as documented in 1985.[25]

Artist Village, Housing Cluster, Charles Correa

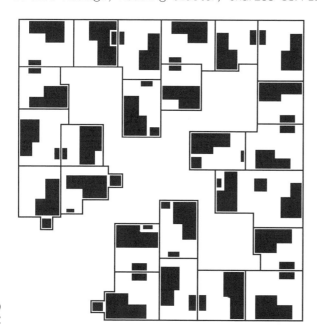

John F.C. Turner + World Bank

John F.C. Turner was the voice of hands-on experience in the developmental self-help movement. Focusing on issues of control, he believed that families left to their own devices often created environments that were more comprehensively successful in addressing their needs than those provided for them by government agencies. Coining the term, "un-aided self-help," Turner was heavily critical of public housing as authoritarian and encouraged a paradigm shift, not in the intention, but in the attitude of self-help, handing the reigns of decision-making over to the users. This lateral advocacy stemmed from his experience beginning three years after his graduation from the Architectural Association (AA) in 1954, when his move to Peru corresponded with a violent earthquake in Arequipa. His practical response to the disaster was an immersive eight-year trial of self-managed home building, one that situated Turner alongside those he was assisting. He spent the next eight years teaching at MIT, publishing an amassment of literature concerning housing policy. During the 1970s and 1980s, Turner had a strong influence on the World Bank's first generation of urban projects, upgrading rather than destroying slums. These slum upgrades in Calcutta, Jakarta and Manila focused on providing clean water and waste management, leaving the improvement of individual homes to the dwellers themselves. Early evaluations of slum upgrades proved wildly successful, affecting millions, with extreme reductions in the incidence and harm of waterborne diseases and an increased investment in home improvement. However, the passage of time placed the sustainability of Turner's theories under scrutiny as conditions eventually worsened and the provided infrastructure was not maintained. Turner is still considered to have spearheaded housing and community development.[26]

Eventual Deterioration: Later Evaluations Show Lack of Maintenance Causing a Decline of Environment and Health, Demonstrating a Delayed Discovery of Projects' Impact.

GIVER  TAKER

Participation/Improvement: Active Improvement of Living Environments; Creation of Businesses and Recreational Facilities. Community Solidarity Formed; Direct Improvements In Health.

GIVER  TAKER

Infrastructural Improvements: Clean Water and Waste Management Provided Directly to Recipients as a Result of Feedback.

GIVER  TAKER

Research/Evaluation: Investment in Theory, Publishing Numerous Studies, Including "Freedom to Build", 1972.

GIVER  TAKER

Enrique Peñalosa + Gates Foundation, Institute for Transportation and Development

Enrique Peñalosa, economist and public administrator, is committed to the improvement of cities, directly engaging with issues of development, transportation, land use and housing. His priorities derive from a conviction that humanism and livability have become essential competitive criteria for economic development. As mayor of Bogota, Colombia from 1998 to 2000, Peñalosa focused on smart, feasible programs for the city, programs that could be realized during his time in office, such as a bicycle path network and pedestrian routes, as well as car-free days. He also improved and multiplied public services such as libraries, parks and public schools. Peñalosa's effectiveness as a politician has made him a valuable resource, serving as advisor to governments across the globe. For the World Bank and the Institute for Transportation and Development Policy, he traveled on missions to Mexico City, Panama City, Lima, New Delhi, Jakarta, Guangzhou, Hong Kong, Surabaya and Yogyakarta, injecting emotion and gusto into discussions of development strategy and policy.[27]

Cameron Sinclair + Architecture for Humanity

Cameron Sinclair has worked to promote an understanding of giving as sharing, where ideas are not treated as personal intellectual property, but knowledge whose value is only realized through its distribution and assistance in the realization of built structures. He has transitioned from architect to social organizer, founding the nonprofit Architecture for Humanity in 1999 with the goal of mobilizing the energy of socially responsible architects through the collective support of an open-source network. Partnering with the community groups, aid organizations, housing developers, government agencies, corporate divisions and foundations like UN Habitat and Relief International, Architecture for Humanity has worked globally, providing disaster relief as well as new infrastructural and development projects. Their post-Katrina reconstruction efforts included an immediate response of four million USD in six months, and the survey of 3,000 houses for damage. His 2006 publication, *Design Like You Give a Damn*, attempts to give a history of socially conscious design in housing, public services and infrastructure. Sinclair has encouraged rapid, networked sharing of not only strategies, but also lessons of trial and error.[28]

Initial Aid Project Implemented With no Prior Knowledge.

Next Project Implemented With Knowledge of Failures and Successes of First Project.

Next Project Implemented With Knowledge of Failures and Successes of First and Second Project.

Mukesh Mehta + Government of Maharashtra, Slum Rehabilitation Authority

Architect and developer Mukesh Mehta understands slums to be one of India's greatest assets. With the US as his inspiration, Mehta believes that what India lacks is a true middle-class to support a consumer society. Benefiting from his father's success in the steel business of India's state of Gujarat, Mehta left India with a degree in architecture and spent over a decade building high-end homes in Long Island's exclusive Nassau County. In 1997, however, he secured a position as chief consultant to the Government of Maharashtra to redevelop Dharavi, redirecting his ambition. Mehta's plan for one of Asia's largest slums is to raze and replace it with a cross-subsidization of free housing with competitively priced housing and commercial space, with chimeras of building a driving range and 120,000-seat cricket stadium. Unlike the trend of self-help schemes, where development is ultimately left to a region's people, Mehta's scheme displays a unique confidence in the market's ability to buoy a community. Rather than stimulate from the ground-up, Mehta wishes to create an attractive vision for external investors. Despite criticism, Mehta has established himself as a self-proclaimed expert of slum rehabilitation, as he has begun accepting similar projects in Hyderabad and Ahmedabad.[29]

Volunteer Aid: Time and Labor

Volunteer's Value

Volunteers may be unpaid, but their work is not without a market value. From formalized institutional volunteering to informal helping, volunteering increases a country's GDP, helps to alleviate social issues and creates many additional benefits, such as helping nonprofit organizations function and providing necessary local services. An individual's decision to volunteer, and how to volunteer is indicative of the value they personally place on their time.

GDP per Capita vs. The Value of The Volunteering Sector in USD
Source: John Hopkins Comparative Nonprofit Sector Project, data ca.1995-2002

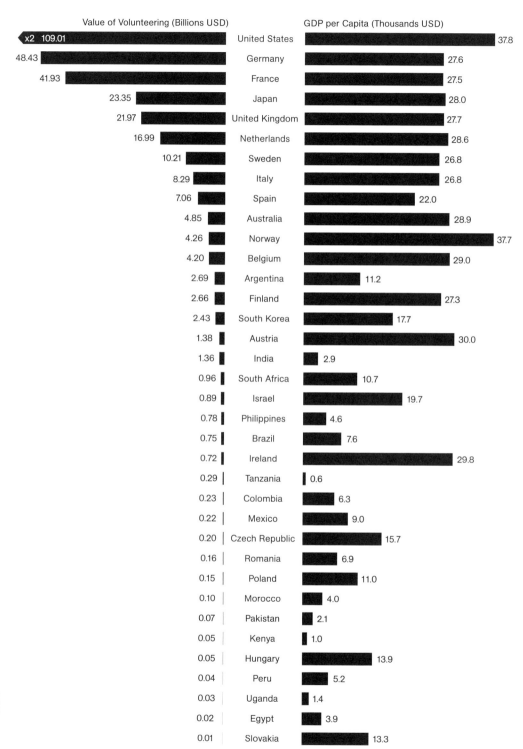

Value of Volunteering (Billions USD)	Country	GDP per Capita (Thousands USD)
x2 109.01	United States	37.8
48.43	Germany	27.6
41.93	France	27.5
23.35	Japan	28.0
21.97	United Kingdom	27.7
16.99	Netherlands	28.6
10.21	Sweden	26.8
8.29	Italy	26.8
7.06	Spain	22.0
4.85	Australia	28.9
4.26	Norway	37.7
4.20	Belgium	29.0
2.69	Argentina	11.2
2.66	Finland	27.3
2.43	South Korea	17.7
1.38	Austria	30.0
1.36	India	2.9
0.96	South Africa	10.7
0.89	Israel	19.7
0.78	Philippines	4.6
0.75	Brazil	7.6
0.72	Ireland	29.8
0.29	Tanzania	0.6
0.23	Colombia	6.3
0.22	Mexico	9.0
0.20	Czech Republic	15.7
0.16	Romania	6.9
0.15	Poland	11.0
0.10	Morocco	4.0
0.07	Pakistan	2.1
0.05	Kenya	1.0
0.05	Hungary	13.9
0.04	Peru	5.2
0.03	Uganda	1.4
0.02	Egypt	3.9
0.01	Slovakia	13.3

Govekar and Govekar's Collective Goods Model

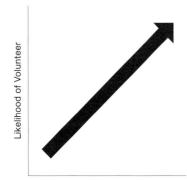

Likelihood of Volunteer

Community's Demand for Charity

Individuals view the time they spend volunteering as having a direct positive influence on the charitable output of an organization, which contributes to an absolute amount of hours.

Govekar and Govekar's Private Goods and Skills Development Theory

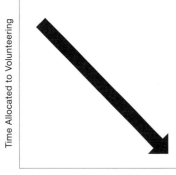

Time Allocated to Volunteering

Wage Earning Opportunities

Despite this, it is assumed that as individuals gain more opportunities to earn money, the time they allocate to volunteering will decrease.

GDP per Capita vs. The Percentage of Adult Population Volunteering
Source: John Hopkins Comparative Nonprofit Sector Project, data ca.1995–2002

% of Adult Population Volunteering		GDP per Capita (Thousands USD)
52	Norway	37.7
30	United Kingdom	27.7
28	Sweden	26.8
23	Uganda	1.4
22	United States	37.8
16	Netherlands	28.6
14	France	27.5
13	Australia	28.9
12	Poland	11.0
11	Ireland	29.8
11	Tanzania	0.6
10	Belgium	29.0
10	Germany	27.6
9	South Africa	10.7
8	Argentina	11.2
8	Austria	30.0
8	Finland	27.3
6	Brazil	7.6
6	Israel	19.7
6	Kenya	1.0
6	Philippines	4.6
5	Colombia	6.3
5	Czech Republic	15.7
5	Peru	5.2
5	Spain	22.0
4	Italy	26.8
4	Morocco	4.0
4	Slovakia	13.3
3	Hungary	13.9
3	South Korea	17.7
2	India	2.9
2	Romania	6.9
1	Egypt	3.9
0.5	Japan	28.0
0.2	Pakistan	2.1

However, in looking at the percentage of adults who volunteer, there is little correlation with individual wealth, or the even potential for individual wealth. This points toward other possible explanations for the prevalence of volunteering.

Value of Volunteering

Realistically, time and money are not so easily inter-changeable. In fact, a large percentage of Americans who partake in charitable activity do more than volun-teer—they give monetary donations as well. Likewise, it is relatively rare that an individual's gift of money is not accompanied by a donation of time. Giving experiences must not all be the same for the giver if both volunteer-ing and donating monetarily are pursued.

Giving and Volunteering as a Percentage of the Adult Population

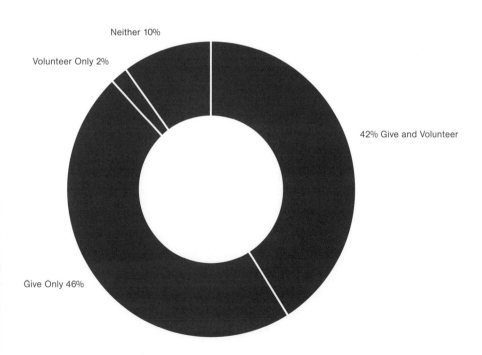

Neither 10%

Volunteer Only 2%

42% Give and Volunteer

Give Only 46%

Contributing Factors to the Amount of Volunteering

Scarcity of Leisure Time

Warm Glow of Time vs. Money

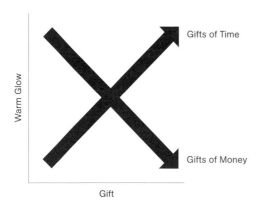

If gifts of time and gifts of money are compatible, and the opportunity cost of leisure equals the price of volunteering, then it would be logical that some people would prefer earning money for their time. This is especially true for those who have highly valued skills and earn a significant wage in the workplace, meaning that a gift a time signals a greater monetary loss, or those that have little free time to give. With this seemingly the case, gifts of time could be rendered completely obsolete, as individuals would spend more time earning money and in turn, increase their gifts of money.

However, this presupposes that an individual finds paid time fulfilling, and would not find other activities more pleasurable. In a 2001 survey, forty-four percent of respondents claimed to give time to charity, with the average time donated being fifteen hours a month. Unlike paid work, volunteering gives an individual a high degree of control over not only where and when they spend their time, but also how, offering a choice in place of the restrictive necessity of paid work.

If the warm-glow of giving an inherent pursuit of human nature, people may give in any situation, particularly if they are in need of mood enhancement. This model does not support the idea that people only give what they have in surplus, or what is at the least cost to them, but rather describes their volunteering as an expression of their social values. Time engaged in addition to money given in support of volunteer activities would contribute a higher reward for the volunteer.

Giving and Volunteering as Percentage of Adult Population (US 2007)
Source: Johns Hopkins Comparative Nonprofit Sector Project, data 1995–200

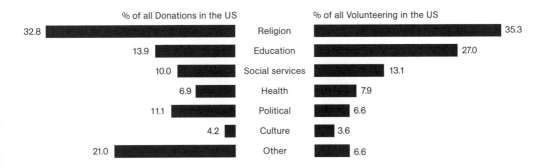

% of all Donations in the US		% of all Volunteering in the US
32.8	Religion	35.3
13.9	Education	27.0
10.0	Social services	13.1
6.9	Health	7.9
11.1	Political	6.6
4.2	Culture	3.6
21.0	Other	6.6

% of Total Volunteering in the US

Activity	%
Other	13.3
Fundraising	11.4
Teaching	10.1
Food Distribution	9.1
General Labor, Transportation	9.0
Equal time among all	8.0
Professional, Management Service	7.9
Athletic Instruction	5.9
Youth Mentoring	5.9
General Office Service	4.6
Arts and Culture Activities	4.3
Welcoming and Guidance	4.2
Clothing, Crafts, Goods Distribution	3.4

Worth of Volunteers

The cost of volunteering can become too high for the volunteer when it diminishes their other opportunities. This holds true especially for organizations that use volunteers. In clear contradiction to the notion that "time is money," many organizations focus their development efforts solely on raising money, not time. Gifts of time, in the form of volunteers, can be seen as a burden. Despite their good intentions, volunteers are perceived as unqualified, untrained and inefficient. Many organizations would rather hire a skilled employee to fulfill their needs rather than utilize a Volunteer Coordinator who would spend both time and money corralling and training additional volunteers.

Percentages of Volunteers vs. Paid Employees by Nonprofit Sector
Source: Johns Hopkins Comparative Nonprofit Sector Project, data 1995–2000

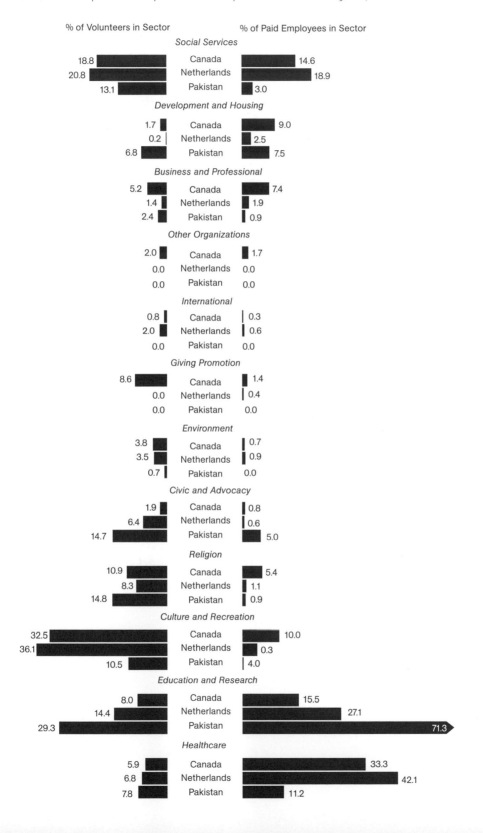

% of Volunteers in Sector   % of Paid Employees in Sector

Social Services

18.8	Canada	14.6
20.8	Netherlands	18.9
13.1	Pakistan	3.0

Development and Housing

1.7	Canada	9.0
0.2	Netherlands	2.5
6.8	Pakistan	7.5

Business and Professional

5.2	Canada	7.4
1.4	Netherlands	1.9
2.4	Pakistan	0.9

Other Organizations

2.0	Canada	1.7
0.0	Netherlands	0.0
0.0	Pakistan	0.0

International

0.8	Canada	0.3
2.0	Netherlands	0.6
0.0	Pakistan	0.0

Giving Promotion

8.6	Canada	1.4
0.0	Netherlands	0.4
0.0	Pakistan	0.0

Environment

3.8	Canada	0.7
3.5	Netherlands	0.9
0.7	Pakistan	0.0

Civic and Advocacy

1.9	Canada	0.8
6.4	Netherlands	0.6
14.7	Pakistan	5.0

Religion

10.9	Canada	5.4
8.3	Netherlands	1.1
14.8	Pakistan	0.9

Culture and Recreation

32.5	Canada	10.0
36.1	Netherlands	0.3
10.5	Pakistan	4.0

Education and Research

8.0	Canada	15.5
14.4	Netherlands	27.1
29.3	Pakistan	71.3

Healthcare

5.9	Canada	33.3
6.8	Netherlands	42.1
7.8	Pakistan	11.2

People generally associate a more pure definition of
volunteering to a provision of societal benefit with a
high cost to the provider, even if the benefit produced
is identical to that of a volunteer who does not endure a
high cost.

Cost/Benefit Analysis (Handy, Cnaan, et al.)

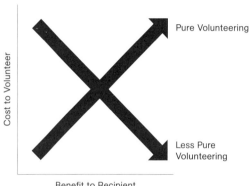

Worth of Volunteering

The volunteer's gift of time and labor can prove as equally generative of Aid Capital as financial gifts. The volunteer labor force comprises a significant portion of the gift economy, largely maintaining momentum through ongoing positive feedback the volunteer. Economists argue that not only do individuals use volunteering as on-the-job training, but they also find compensation in the psychological gain that is derived from giving. Such capital influences self-esteem and enhances individual self-worth. The return on spent Aid Capital for the volunteer occurs in real time. Time spent volunteering can also be more concretely to the volunteer's advantage—in the display of morals or in the chance to gain knowledge and to build a skill set. The opportunity for individuals to socialize with other volunteers and with recipients may be an even greater reward than receiving some form of material compensation for time spent volunteering.

Brown and Zahrly's Social Theory of Volunteering

Individual's Desire to Volunteer

Opportunity to Socialize

International Volunteer Levels in the Cultural Sector

Source: Johns Hopkins Comparative Nonprofit Sector Project, data 1995–2000

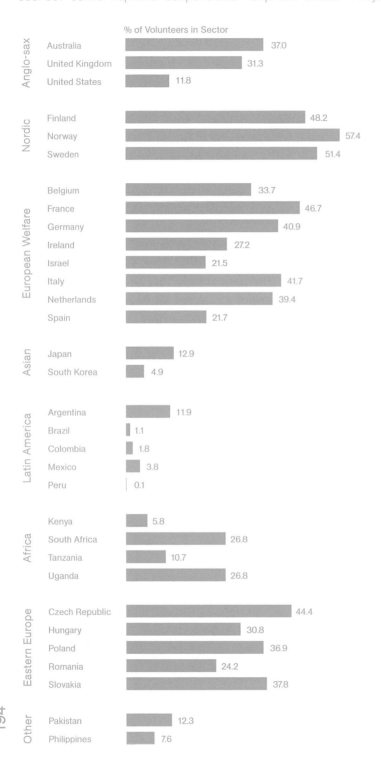

% of Volunteers in Sector

Anglo-sax
- Australia — 37.0
- United Kingdom — 31.3
- United States — 11.8

Nordic
- Finland — 48.2
- Norway — 57.4
- Sweden — 51.4

European Welfare
- Belgium — 33.7
- France — 46.7
- Germany — 40.9
- Ireland — 27.2
- Israel — 21.5
- Italy — 41.7
- Netherlands — 39.4
- Spain — 21.7

Asian
- Japan — 12.9
- South Korea — 4.9

Latin America
- Argentina — 11.9
- Brazil — 1.1
- Colombia — 1.8
- Mexico — 3.8
- Peru — 0.1

Africa
- Kenya — 5.8
- South Africa — 26.8
- Tanzania — 10.7
- Uganda — 26.8

Eastern Europe
- Czech Republic — 44.4
- Hungary — 30.8
- Poland — 36.9
- Romania — 24.2
- Slovakia — 37.8

Other
- Pakistan — 12.3
- Philippines — 7.6

International Volunteer Levels in the Environmental Sector
Source: Johns Hopkins Comparative Nonprofit Sector Project, data 1995–2000

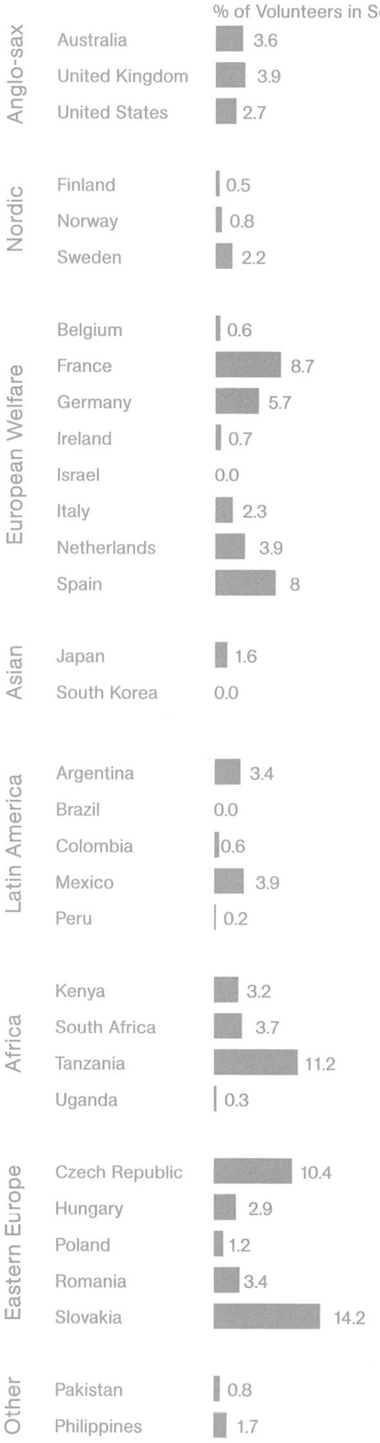

% of Volunteers in Sector

Anglo-sax

Australia   3.6
United Kingdom   3.9
United States   2.7

Nordic

Finland   0.5
Norway   0.8
Sweden   2.2

European Welfare

Belgium   0.6
France   8.7
Germany   5.7
Ireland   0.7
Israel   0.0
Italy   2.3
Netherlands   3.9
Spain   8

Asian

Japan   1.6
South Korea   0.0

Latin America

Argentina   3.4
Brazil   0.0
Colombia   0.6
Mexico   3.9
Peru   0.2

Africa

Kenya   3.2
South Africa   3.7
Tanzania   11.2
Uganda   0.3

Eastern Europe

Czech Republic   10.4
Hungary   2.9
Poland   1.2
Romania   3.4
Slovakia   14.2

Other

Pakistan   0.8
Philippines   1.7

International Volunteer Levels in the Social Sector
Source: Johns Hopkins Comparative Nonprofit Sector Project, data 1995–2000

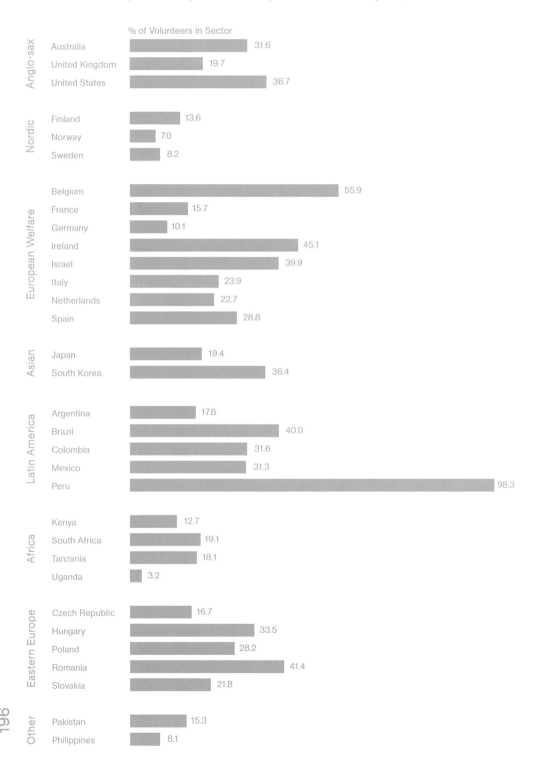

% of Volunteers in Sector

Anglo-sax
- Australia — 31.6
- United Kingdom — 19.7
- United States — 36.7

Nordic
- Finland — 13.6
- Norway — 7.0
- Sweden — 8.2

European Welfare
- Belgium — 55.9
- France — 15.7
- Germany — 10.1
- Ireland — 45.1
- Israel — 39.9
- Italy — 23.9
- Netherlands — 22.7
- Spain — 28.8

Asian
- Japan — 19.4
- South Korea — 36.4

Latin America
- Argentina — 17.8
- Brazil — 40.0
- Colombia — 31.6
- Mexico — 31.3
- Peru — 98.3

Africa
- Kenya — 12.7
- South Africa — 19.1
- Tanzania — 18.1
- Uganda — 3.2

Eastern Europe
- Czech Republic — 16.7
- Hungary — 33.5
- Poland — 28.2
- Romania — 41.4
- Slovakia — 21.8

Other
- Pakistan — 15.3
- Philippines — 8.1

International Volunteer Levels in the Development Sector
Source: Johns Hopkins Comparative Nonprofit Sector Project, data 1995–2000

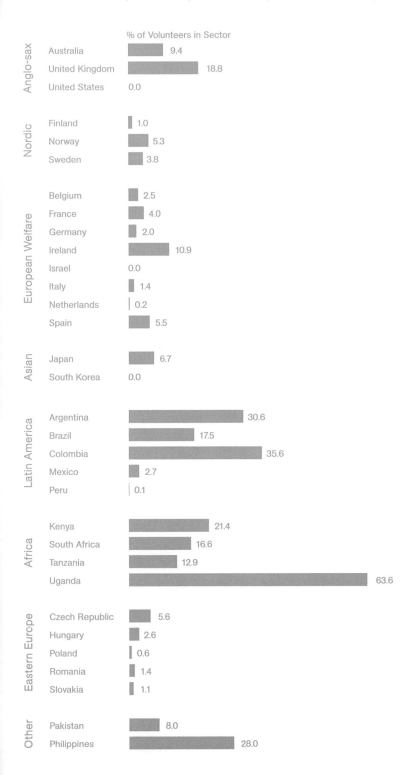

% of Volunteers in Sector

Anglo-sax
- Australia — 9.4
- United Kingdom — 18.8
- United States — 0.0

Nordic
- Finland — 1.0
- Norway — 5.3
- Sweden — 3.8

European Welfare
- Belgium — 2.5
- France — 4.0
- Germany — 2.0
- Ireland — 10.9
- Israel — 0.0
- Italy — 1.4
- Netherlands — 0.2
- Spain — 5.5

Asian
- Japan — 6.7
- South Korea — 0.0

Latin America
- Argentina — 30.6
- Brazil — 17.5
- Colombia — 35.6
- Mexico — 2.7
- Peru — 0.1

Africa
- Kenya — 21.4
- South Africa — 16.6
- Tanzania — 12.9
- Uganda — 63.6

Eastern Europe
- Czech Republic — 5.6
- Hungary — 2.6
- Poland — 0.6
- Romania — 1.4
- Slovakia — 1.1

Other
- Pakistan — 8.0
- Philippines — 28.0

Givingness is Next to Godliness

Nuns are givers, but givers of a higher order, whose formalized commitment to what might be called an "economy of spirituality" distinguishes them from other aid workers. They have a different relationship to altruism, as their gift is one of their lives to God, after giving such they become his mere blessed tools. They are full-time professionals whose seclusion from everyday life creates a unique relation between dedication, work and reward. Nuns are inducted by a process of sacrifice and dedication, requiring their relinquishment of normative entitlements like wage labor, possession, career mobility (or any possibility of power positions), sexuality and sex, substance use and other freedoms of dress and diet as perceived obstacles to a heightened religiosity of unequivocal focus. This withdrawal from society may be considered extreme from a conventional social perspective but is founded on a paradoxical but fundamentally necessary distance from the very object of work commitment. The distance enforces and cultivates the extraordinary closeness of the subject with God.

Growth, in the cloisters, is limited to that of the spirit, presumably unlimited. The church provides the nun's sustenance and care, and her productive labor is engaged to spiritual ends exclusively, meditatively and generously. The motion of all work is outward, and what is enjoyed as a return is precisely its material lack. In its stead, surrogate compensation is "divined," so to speak, through the enhanced richness of one's relations with God.

The relation of the giving and recipient parties is thus mediated by a conceptual-spiritual abstraction, structured as follows. God, as the creator and savior, is positioned as the original and ultimate giver, both through creation of the world and through the gift of eternal life made available to all baptized believers through Christ's own death. By the taking of vows and the dedication to those vows, nuns position themselves as conduits for God's generosity to be made manifest in the material world. In this case, they may give gifts as worldly agents in God's name. This situates the nun as a medium of sorts, someone who has given away everything in order to give herself to God. This protocol of giving paradoxically requires having nothing left to give, being possession-less and self-less, one with God.

The nun's faith in God's benevolence and active awareness of suffering on Earth allows her to be God's agent. Faith is not required on the part of a recipient. From the nun's perspective, a recipient can receive the nun's gifts of aid or effects of prayer, knowingly or unknowingly, faithful or faithless. Regardless of the recipient's religious beliefs, through giving, the nun receives grace and the reaffirms her certainty of acting as God's direct agent, God's power flowing through her actions. The gift is given "in good faith."

This quality of giving as a given itself can be understood as an affirmation of the distance between the life-realms of the involved subjects; the community of the worldly vessels for God's work intervening in the secular world from which God is occluded. Were no such divide to be conceived, no blessed intervention would be necessary or possible. This is especially true of a gift given so freely, carried by belief from an economy of spiritual reward into the larger monetary-material system. But it must be remembered that the freedom of this gift to move across this boundary is had in the first place by boundary's very demarcation—that is, by the intervening intermediary of God in the relationship between the committed religious and the lay faithful. A loving, beneficent God thus absorbs any mutual self-interest that would economically bind giver and receiver. The nun is merely God's channel.

The convent and the habit are two devices that protect nuns from integration with and misrecognition as lay people. The convent physically isolates them; the habit marks them as other. These devices

A nun stands as a landmark for a Los Angeles marathon.

would seem essential to the act of giving depending on the nun's identity as a special channel to the divine. However, in practice, convents and habits are seen increasingly as formal obstacles to effectiveness in gift implementation. Being prevented from direct contact with people in need may unnecessarily restrict acts of help to prayer alone rather than additional direct intervention. Habits can interfere with volunteer work by their ungainly arrangement and by inspiring aversion in potential beneficiaries. As a result, not all nuns in the contemporary world remain cloistered and wear habits, many choosing to live in the outside community and wear clothing that bears little distinction from that worn by the general populace. This has become a serious point of contention between the Vatican and some American orders.

Caritas is a foundational principle of love common to all Catholics (and Christians, generally), but its implementation reflects an assumption of fundamental difference between giver and recipient. Caritas typically finds expression by nuns in an overarching concern for the good of humanity. But it is unclear whether empathy is re-quired in order to achieve God's intended results. What is the significance of the difference or similarity of the people involved in the expression of this religious love? Theoretically, a committed nun has little personal experience of society's ills, even of poverty itself, experienced by the nun not as a negative but as a gift to god. Though one would not suggest that nuns should directly dabble in broken marriages and addiction, nuns are nonetheless expected to be able to counsel and heal those suffering under these pressures.

It is felt by many that the Vatican would have nuns "re-retreat" from practical work in society and focus their energies once again on the power of appeals to God or saints for assistance through prayer. This implicitly cuts out the recipient from any interpersonal interaction, use of belief in God exclusively as a sort of satellite for the reflection, harnessing, and targeting of goodwill. Such a total rejection of interaction with the world beyond the cloister would amount to a loss of the immediate practical relief given through the nuns' gifts, those gifts themselves understood as realizations of God's will. If her personal understanding of her beliefs compels her to help others by methods other than solitary prayer, does her acting on this qualify as disobedience, if the Vatican orders otherwise? If she already understands that a profound cognitive separation between her and those she gives to is part of what makes her work successful, does the enforcement of a physical separation from them follow as necessary?

Above: An Ecuadorian nun greets a lay faithful arriving for missionary work.
Below: A group of nuns await a bus in New York.

Two nuns en route to their convent, goods in tow.

Confidence and Volunteering

Some theorists argue that an individual's confidence in an organization is directly related to the likelihood that they will volunteer for that organization. Others argue against this theory, stating that only the inherent confidence of religious individuals in their religious organizations positively impacts their desire to volunteer. The act of volunteering for an organization one is unfamiliar with exposes the volunteer to the organization and problem area in unpredictable ways. The phenomenon of volunteers having little knowledge of the larger framing of their activity may be evidence of the fact that volunteers are not even expecting, or more precisely, waiting to receive information as to their effectiveness to be able to enjoy the experience of volunteering. The element of self-gratification found when volunteering may outpace any external information, such as the results of the organization at large and how it might be differentiated from other organizations.

Bowman's Hypothesis on Confidence and Volunteering

Hypothesis 1
Expect less volunteering from those with less confidence in charitable organizations. Rational individuals may feel as though the time they might spend volunteering would be wasted if they have no confidence in the organization, that one's time could be better spent providing public good in a different way.

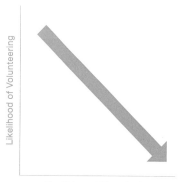

Hypothesis 2

Asking an individual to volunteer increases the chances that they will, regardless of their confidence in the organization. Those who start with lower confidence will experience a greater increase in confidence after volunteering than those who started with higher confidence. This exhibits the principle of diminishing marginal utility.

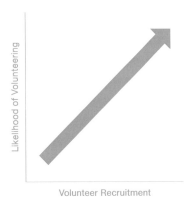

Hypothesis 3

Once affiliated with an organization, volunteering increases the probability that an individual will have a high level of confidence in charitable institutions as a general category.

7
Feedback

Information Value

After World War II, foreign aid debates focused on the balance between basic needs and economic development, measured in growth of GDP per capita. Quantifiable economic growth was the singular concern of giver countries, as it was thought vital for lesser-developed countries to self-govern effectively. Foreign aid could boost a nation through the lower stages of development, when the resulting economic activity and prosperity could then (and only then) be a catalyst for social progress—a "trickle-down" effect. Social benefit could best be measured through economic statistics, the quantifiable consumption of material goods and services. By the 1970s, most economists did recognize the need for indices other than economic ones; Robert McNamara stated in 1971 that, "[d]evelopment has for too long been expressed simply in terms of growth of output. There is now emerging the awareness that the availability of work, the distribution of income, and the quality of life are equally important measures of development."[1]

Although this acknowledgment did little to adjust formal development criteria, the aid discussion itself became nuanced, incorporating the relationship between quality of life and economic power. How should aid be calibrated to address both the daily quality of life of the people and the economic health of their country? How did these factors relate over time and how could they be objectively evaluated? The indicators appeared closely correlated in some studies, while in others distinctly not. For instance, Zuvekas found that economic growth could occur without noticeably increasing social indicators, while Streeten strongly suggested a "trickle-up" system, where human capital achieves a productivity potential necessary for growth.[2] Overall, however, the discussion was disappointingly inconclusive. GDP remained the dominant criterion, with official economic statistics providing the primary feedback guiding foreign aid policy decisions.

Sectors of Aid Allocation, 1975–2005
Source: OECD

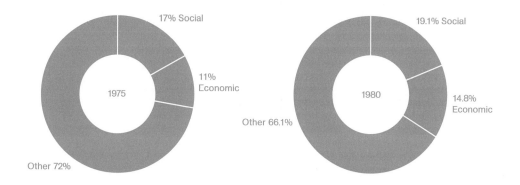

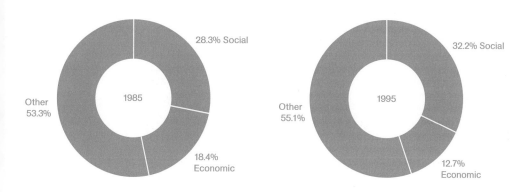

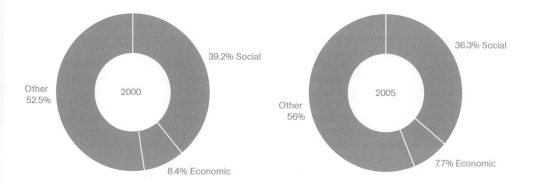

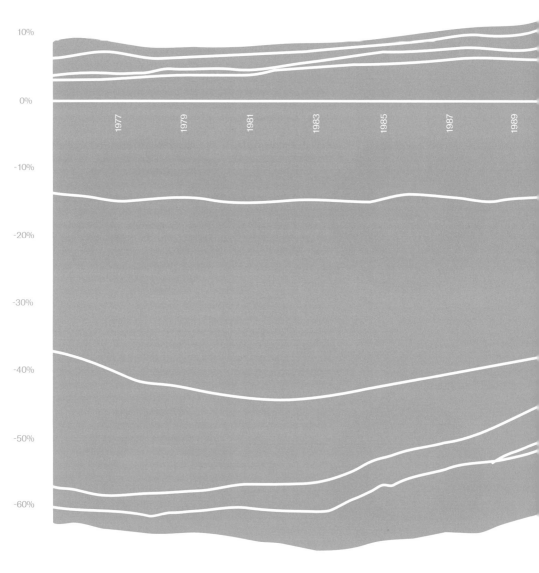

30%

20%

10%

0%

1977   1979   1981   1983   1985   1987   1989

-10%

-20%

-30%

-40%

-50%

-60%

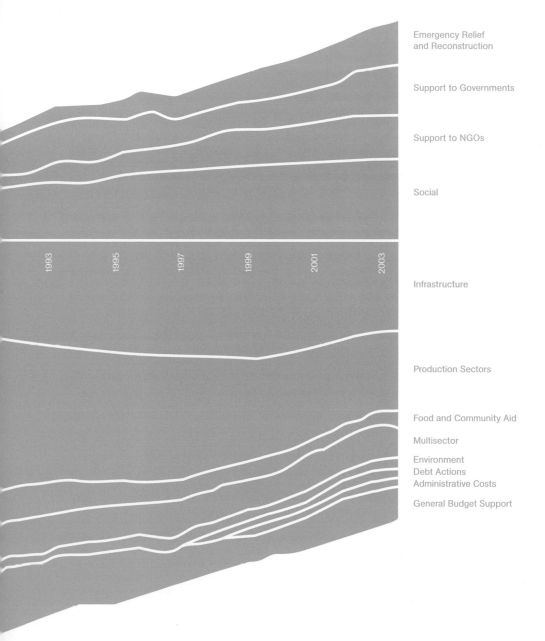

Emergency Relief
and Reconstruction

Support to Governments

Support to NGOs

Social

1993   1995   1997   1999   2001   2003

Infrastructure

Production Sectors

Food and Community Aid

Multisector

Environment
Debt Actions
Administrative Costs

General Budget Support

The condition of available housing also received an increasing level of attention after World War II. In the post-war period, housing was seen as merely a social concern and categorized as a pure cost with a negative effect on economic growth. Further, aid workers found the international building industry to be archaic, unskilled and unable to adapt to their methods of working. Consistent with the times, large-scale production methods like prefabrication were preferred.[3] Thus, from whichever prospering nation they happened to be headquartered, aid agencies would ship one giant kit of design documents, engineers, workers and building materials. This practice effectively prevented construction from engaging the local economy of the recipient country.

Self-help was promoted successfully, as previously shown by the number of architects and urban planners who rallied behind the idea, as a solution to aided housing's problems. Rather than the prefab kit with labor included, efforts were made to engage the population while also keeping down costs. Yet, economists disagreed with this change in strategy, charging that it merely temporarily occupied the underemployed and that a more sustainable employment solution should also be found.[4] In a 1958 report to the UN, economists began to describe health as impacting economic growth, nutrition and housing grouped under this heading. In 1964, Gary Becker advocated for the idea of human capital—the innate economic potential of investments in such areas as education and health (things that have no value when separated from the person to which they belong). For instance, housing built in the wake of WWII was becoming an established point of reference, producing new data for the development aid community that revealed aid housing's long-term positive effect on local economies. In 1973, even the resolutely fiscally minded World Bank began funding housing projects in developing countries.

Indicative of shifting priorities was the turn of attention away from the rural sector to urban environments as urban centers gained increasing economic importance during periods of modernization and industrialization (1960s–1970s). The United States Agency for International Development (USAID), a self-defined "rural development agency" stated in 1984 that "[i]t is our opinion that the congressional mandate to aid the 'poor majority' means aid to whoever is determined by USAID, in its Agency expertise, to be the poor majority, be they urban or rural poor."[5] This has a direct material impact; the population growth of urban areas has been cited as a reason to further reallocate resources away from the rural sector.

Urban vs. Rural Population in Developing Countries
Source: Pinstrup-Andersen et. al. (1999)

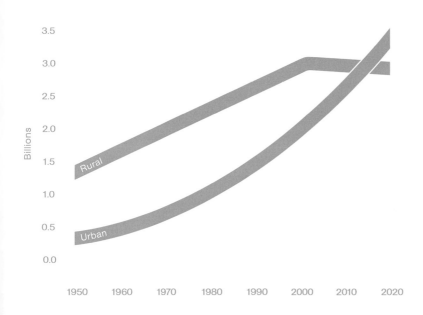

Urban and rural are not so easily interchangeable. Issues of urban poverty are complicated by spatial considerations and lack of access, requiring much adjustment to former primarily rural-targeted poverty alleviation strategies. Givers have realized the intricacies of addressing an urban environment, which presents the challenge of a large wealth gap making it impossible to apply even treatment of all inhabitants in need. The agent of this split is the slum, the ever-expanding location of urban poverty. Slum dwellers are frequently in need of sanitation infrastructure, water, education, secure housing and in some cases employment, even through all already exists, if not in abundance, in their same city. While new urban conurbations are worrisome to aid agencies on the basis of standards of living, they are also viewed as sites of significant economic potential, fueling an intense interest in their development. As greater and greater numbers of former rural inhabitants moved to cities, the urban environment came to symbolize in the aid community the collapse of the human and the economic into a single geographic and conceptual territory.

The Human Development Index

The discussion of aid sector interdependence was resolved by focusing efforts on developing a methodological merging of the social and the economic into a single measurement. Such a measurement was intended to create a persuasive alternative to the GDP feedback model and at last direct aid attention to the actual lives of people. The Human Development Index (HDI), designed to measure length of life, health, knowledge and standard of living, was put forth by the UN in 1990. The HDI would yearly collect and tabulate data from three indices—life expectancy, education and GDP per capita-purchasing power—providing a normalized, working data set. The raw numbers could then be rigorously evaluated and reformulated to correct for errors and inconsistencies inevitable in a statistical project of this range and scope. *Human Development Reports* analyzing particular aspects of the HDI continue to be published yearly by the United Nations and are responsible for the familiar categorization of "developed," "developing" and "least developed" countries. *The Human Development Reports*, each with a particular focus on a pressing issue have displayed a bold vision, a self-proclaimed "paradigm shift…[creating] indices that measure human freedoms."[6]

These annual reports quickly became dominant in aid circles. The first report in 1990 was aptly titled *Concept and Measurement of Human Development*, 1995's looked at *Gender and Human Development*, 2001's considered *Making New Technologies Work for Human Development* and 2008's took on *Fighting Climate Change: Human Solidarity in a Divided World*. Some reports were controversial, such as 1996's *Economic Growth and Human Development*, which stated definitively that economic growth was not an end in and of itself—only a means to achieve human development.[7] While obviously incapable of providing small project—or program—specific feedback, the index is intended to be responsive to large initiatives, influxes of aid and the cumulative effect of the entire giving community, from NGO donors to ODA contributions. The HDI has itself developed, now including three additional indices: two tracking gender issues and a third that assesses poverty.

Criticisms of the annual reports' accuracy and elegance of resolution still abound. The primary criticism is stagnancy. By its own assessment, the HDI is limited in the indicators it uses; without clear justification all are given equal statistical weight. As well, the "goalposts" are somewhat arbitrary. For instance, life expectancy as measured by the HDI is bounded by a minimum of twenty-five and a maximum of eighty-five years. In reporting data by country, any inequalities unequally distributed in the nation's interior become flattened. There is no adjustment for resource allocation. Further, reporting of data is necessarily uneven in terms of thoroughness and consistency across countries. There are some larger, persistent concerns that the HDI hopes to soon address and incorporate—but has not yet. These include gauges of the degrees of political freedom and violations of human rights, as well as measurements of environmental degradation and resource utilization. In comparison with permanent features such as the presence of oil reserves, there are other, more localized, comparatively short-term occurrences that the system does not account for, such as war, natural disaster, drastic political shifts or serious civil unrest.

While criticisms clearly point out vital weaknesses, the larger problem lies not with the Index itself per se, but with how it is interpreted—namely, that it is not. The Human Development Reports are intended for policy formulation, yet the HDI is obviously not capable of communicating nuanced information given its minimalist, utilitarian design. Beyond the normative concerns associated with a typical glossing over of complex issues, the HDI emphasizes an idea of need over that of want. Bryan Caplan points out that the HDI, "effectively proclaims an 'end of history' where Scandinavia is the pinnacle of human achievement… Scandinavia comes out on top according to the HDI because the HDI is basically a measure of how Scandinavian your country is."[8]

Foreign Direct Investment

It is precisely this issue—local variations ignored by statistical measurements—that has reopened the debate about the sectorial application of aid. From an economist's perspective, globalization throughout the 1990s contributed to the increasing possibility of public-private partnerships in large-scale aid projects. Aid Capital could thus be said to have increased in this area. In particular, multilateral institutions promoted this type of development, inspired perhaps most strongly by the ineffectiveness of official government-led aid reforms.

The private sector offered developing countries a primarily economic alternative to official aid, unlike NGO aid flows that tended strongly towards social concerns. One of the most promising appeared to be foreign direct investment (FDI): the facilitation of material business investments in such things as a factory in a country other that of the investor. These arrangements are not aid as it has been understood. No investor would suggest that their actions are intended to be as beneficial for the host country as for the investor. Nevertheless, FDI offers a degree of freedom of choice and control to a developing country beyond what is possible with official aid channels. They can initiate partnerships, have control over which businesses are allowed to operate, and ultimately, dictate the terms of each arrangement.

As has been suggested by World Bank research, certain countries interested in pursuing FDI lack the necessary large-scale infrastructure—transportation or communications, for example—to be attractive to foreign investors. This raises a pivotal question: if it is a preferential arrangement for certain countries, should said countries be able to request official aid in the form of infrastructural investment, essentially classic economic development investment? Further, should giver countries be charged with the task of incorporating the fulfillment of developing countries' desires, this even taking precedence over the giver country's own logic or preferences?

FDI has distinct problems of its own, which the OECD lists as: "a deterioration of the balance of payments as profits are repatriated, a lack of positive linkages with local communities, the potentially harmful environmental impact of FDI, especially in the extractive and heavy industries, social disruptions of accelerated commercialization in less developed countries [and] an increasing dependence on internationally operating enterprises as representing a loss of political sovereignty."[9] Further the host country may not be in a position to take advantage of the technology or knowledge present at the foreign business, despite proximity.

However, one of the greatest challenges of FDI, as a strategy, is its linkage to the market economy. While this can provide useful resources and allows recipient countries to operate in a contractual, rather than a giving-taking, environment, the market leaves weaker economies at the mercy of its inherent volatility. In this sense, investors remain unconcerned with the issues that preoccupy givers. In an FDI scenario, there is no ulterior or extra-economic commitment to a project, nor to the project's local beneficiaries unless they also happen to be stockholders.

Rather than through aid channels, any feedback from an FDI project or program cycles into the global market, which has only one preoccupation. Abrupt decisions might be made by investors to reallocate resources on the receipt of negative projections. The east Asian economies, for example, that had grown so strongly after the 1960s were nearly undone by a two-year recession. The attentions of the market are flattering, but they are also fickle. No matter how seemingly warm the embrace, they never enter into a long-term commitment without an exit plan.

Slow Giving

Giving, despite its variations over time, moves at a practically glacial pace compared to the speed of the market. Giving—with its managed, determined flows—reveals itself to be a long-term, conservative practice, for better or worse.

Despite new methods of transference or connectivity, giving provides a necessary element of stability in the realm of global exchange. At times, the characteristic of being slow to adapt can be beneficial. Giving becomes a constant that coexists with other more dynamic processes that pay less attention to qualitative human conditions. Such aspects of the complex dynamics of capital, such as the financial markets, have the useful capacity to rapidly adjust in order to be most efficient. While aid should in no way strive for inefficiency, neither should it divest itself of the long-term protection and assurance it provides.

Notes to the Text

Notes to Chapter 1: *Given*, pp 9–29

1 Angie Debo, *The Rise and Fall of the Choctaw Republic* (Norman: University of Oklahoma Press, 1934).
2 http://www.msnbc.msn.com/id/32532398/ns/us_news-wonderful_world/.
3 *World Cruising Club Magazine*, 22, (Middletown, Rhode Island: Bonnier, 2007).
4 William Chester Jordan, *The Great Famine: Northern Europe in the Early Fourteenth Century* (Princeton: Princeton University Press, 1997).
5 *Harriet Tubman*, in the PBS Resource Bank: http://www.pbs.org/wgbh/aia/part4/4p1535.html.
6 Kathryn Spink, *Mother Teresa: A Complete Authorized Biography* (New York: Harper Collins Publishers, 1997).
7 Vivienne Walt, "Sweden: A Haven from war confronts the price of generosity," *Time Magazine*, March 02, 2007, Online Edition. http://www.time.com/time/magazine/article/0,9171,1595247,00.html.
8 Jacob Neusner, Bruce D. Chilton, *Altruism in World Religions* (Washington D.C.: Georgetown University Press, 2005).
9 http://www.cnn.com/2009/LIVING/wayoflife/06/28/elderly.blood.donor/index.html
10 "$63,441,995 Received by Community Chests," *New York Times*, December 7, 1931: 8.
11 Robert Hamlett Bremner, *Giving: Charity and Philanthropy in History* (Edison: Transaction Publishers, 1994).
12 The History Channel: http://www.history.com/this-day-in-history.do?action=Article&id=52887.
13 David Murray, *Indian Giving: Economies of Power in Early Indian-White Exchanges* (Amherst: University of Massachusetts Press, 2000).
14 Londa Schiebinger, *Plants and Empire* (Cambridge: Harvard University Press, 2004).
15 Kevin Fasick and Tom Namako, "MTA fines if you don't give a sit," *New York Post*, June 18, 2009, Regional News, Online Edition. New York Post online: http://www.nypost.com/seven/06182009/news/regionalnews/mta_fines_if_you_dont_give_a_sit_174822.htm.
16 Ali Kriscenski, "HEINEKEN WOBO: The brick that holds beer," *Inhabitat* (Weblog), posted October 11, 2007. http://www.inhabitat.com/2007/10/11/heineken-wobo-the-brick-that-holds-beer/.
17 Walter W. Powell and Richard Steinberg, ed., *The Non-profit Sector: A Research Handbook* (New Haven: Yale University Press, 2006).
18 The Nun Study at the University Minnesota: http://www.healthstudies.umn.edu/nunstudy/.
19 Jacob Roggeveen, "June 1722, the Dutch 'Discovery'," in *'First Contacts' in Polynesia: The Samoan Case* (1722–1848): Western misunderstandings about sexuality and divinity, Louis-Antoine de Bougainville, Jacob Roggeveen (Canberra: Australian National University E Press), http://epress.anu.edu.au/first_contacts/mobile_devices/index.html.
20 Eduardo Porter, "Radiohead's Warm Glow," *New York Times*, October 14, 2007, Editorial, Online Edition. http://www.nytimes.com/2007/10/14/opinion/14sun3.html.
21 Walter W. Powell and Richard Steinberg, ed., *The Non-profit Sector: A Research Handbook* (New Haven: Yale University Press, 2006).
22 *Courier-Post* online: http://www.courierpostonline.com/apps/pbcs.dll/article?AID=/20071226/NEWS01/712260334/1006.
23 Chris Brook, *K Foundation Burn a Million Quid* (London: Ellipsis London, 1998).
24 "Useless teddy bear – Kadirgamar," *BBC Sinhala.com*, March 17, 2005, Online. http://www.bbc.co.uk/sinhala/news/story/2005/03/050317_laxman_london.shtml.
25 *Virtualology: A Virtual Education Project*, s.v. "John D. Rockefeller." http://www.johndrockefeller.org/.
26 Virgil, *The Aeneid*. http://classics.mit.edu/Virgil/aeneid.html
27 United States Department of Agriculture's Food and Nutrition Service website: http://www.fns.usda.gov/pd/34SNAPmonthly.htm.
28 Ibid.
29 Robert P. Connolly, "UMass Trustees Unanimously Rescind Robert Mugabe Degree," *UMass Amherst Office of News & Media Relations*, June 12, 2008, Online. http://www.umass.edu/newsoffice/newsreleases/articles/76038.php.
30 Madeline Ellis, "Washington Adopts Death With Dignity Act Legalizing Assisted Suicide" *Health News*, March 3, 2009, Online Edition. http://www.healthnews.com/medical-updates/washington-adopts-death-with-dignity-act-legalizing-assisted-suicide-2724.html.
31 *T-Shirt Travels*, directed by Shantha Bloemen (2001; San Francisco, CA: Independent Television Service).
32 Carnegie Medals of Philanthropy: http://www.carnegiemedals.org/news/new_awardees.html.

33   David Murray, *Indian Giving: Economies
      of Power in Early Indian-White Exchanges*
      (Amherst: University of Massachusetts Press,
      2000).

34   "Pixar fulfills dying girl's wish to see 'Up',"
      MSNBC, June 19, 2009, Entertainment
      Section, Online. http://www.msnbc.msn.com/
      id/31448115/ns/entertainment-movies/.

35   Stephen Kinzer, *All the Shah's Men: An
      American Coup and the Roots of Middle East
      Terror* (Hoboken: John Wiley & Sons, 2008).

36   Mumin Shakirov, "Chukotka's Smitten With
      Roman Abramovich," *The St. Petersburg
      Times*, Aug 7, 2001, Online Edition. http://
      www.sptimes.ru/index.php?action_
      id=2&story_id=4993.

Notes to Chapter 2: *Motives*, pp 31–57

1   *Stanford Encyclopedia of Philosophy Online*,
      s.v. "David Hume." http://plato.stanford.edu/
      entries/hume/ and L. A. Selby-Brigge, ed.,
      Enquiry Concerning the Principles of Morals,
      (Oxford: Clarendon Press, 1975): 298.

2   *Stanford Encyclopedia of Philosophy Online*,
      s.v. "Biological Altruism." http://plato.stanford.
      edu/entries/altruism-biological/.

3   Phillipe Fontaine, "Who is Afraid of the
      Past? Economic Theorists and Historians
      of Economics on Altruism," *Journal of the
      History of Economic Thought* (1998), http://
      eh.net/pipermail/hes/1998-October/005423.
      html. See also, Phillipe Fontaine, "From
      Philanthropy to Altruism: Incorporating
      Unselfish Behavior into Economics," History
      of Political Economy, Vol. 39 (2007): 1–46.

4   Herbert Gintis, Samuel Bowles, Robert Boyd,
      and Ernst Fehr, "Explaining Altruistic Behavior
      in Humans," *Evolution and Human Behavior,*
      Vol. 24 (2003): 153–172.

5   John Stuart Mill, and George Sher, eds.
      Utilitarianism (London: Hackett Pub Co, 2nd
      edition, 2002).

6   Peter Singer, "Famine, Affluence, and
      Morality," *Philosophy and Public Affairs*,
      Vol.1, No.1 (Spring 1972): 229–243. See also,
      Peter Singer, Practical Ethics (Cambridge:
      Cambridge University Press, 1993).

7   Adam Smith, *An Inquiry Into the Nature and
      Causes of the Wealth of Nations* (1776). http://
      www.adamsmith.org/smith/won-
      index.htm.

8   Marcel Mauss, "Essai sur le don. Forme
      et raison de l'échange dans les sociétés
      archaïques," *l'Année Sociologique*, seconde
      série, 1923–1924, translated into English as
      *The Gift: The Form and Reason for Exchange
      in Archaic Societies*, trans. W.D. Halls (New
      York: Norton, 2000).

Notes to Chapter 3: *History*, pp 59–75

1   Noriko Kurushima, "Marriage and Female
      Inheritance in Medieval Japan," *International
      Journal of Asian Studies*, Vol.1, No.2
      (2004): 223.

2   Alan Macfarlane, "The Mystery of Property:
      Inheritance and Industrialization in England
      and Japan," in C.M.Hann ed., *Property
      Relations. Renewing the Anthropological
      Tradition* (Cambridge: Cambridge University
      Press, 1998): 119.

3   Osamu Saito, "Land, Labour, and Market
      Forces in Tokugawa Japan," *Continuity and
      Change*, Vol. 24 (Cambridge: Cambridge
      University Press, 2009): 171.

4   Noriko Kurushima, "Marriage and Female
      Inheritance in Medieval Japan," *International
      Journal of Asian Studies*, Vol.1, No.2
      (2004): 224.

5   Evelyn Cecil, *Primogeniture* (London: J.
      Murray, 1895): 128.

6   Masao Takagi, "Landholdings and the Family
      Life Cycle in Traditional Japan," *Continuity
      and Change*, Vol. 15 (Cambridge: Cambridge
      University Press, 2000): 51.

7   Masao Takagi, "Succession and the Death of
      the Household Head in Early Modern Japan,"
      Continuity and Change, Vol. 13 (Cambridge:
      Cambridge University Press, 1998): 144.

8   Motoyasu Takahashi, "Family Continuity in
      England and Japan," *Continuity and Change*,
      Vol. 22 (Cambridge: Cambridge University
      Press, 2007): 206.

9   Alan Macfarlane, "The Mystery of Property:
      Inheritance and Industrialization in England
      and Japan," in C. M. Hann ed., *Property
      Relations. Renewing the Anthropological
      Tradition* (Cambridge: Cambridge University
      Press, 1998): 121.

10   Anne Elizabeth Conger McCants, *Civic
      Charity in a Golden Age* (Urbana: University
      of Illinois Press, 1997): 192.

11   Max Weber, and Talcott Parsons, trans., The
      Protestant Ethic and the Spirit of Capitalism
      (New York: Charles Scribner's Sons, 1958).

12   Marco Van Leeuwen, et al, "Giving in the
      Golden Age: presentation of a new research
      project," *Paper for the Fourth Flemish-Dutch
      Conference of the economic and social
      history of the Low Countries before 1850*
      (January 2009): 3. http://www.lowcountries.
      nl/papers2009/papers2009_vanleeuwen.pdf.

13   Ibid, 5.

14   Geoffrey Parker, *Europe in Crisis*, 1598–1648
      (Ithaca: Cornell University Press, 1979): 15.

15   Martin Fitzpatrick, Peter Jones, Christa
      Knellwolf, and Iain McCalman, eds., *The
      Enlightenment World* (New York: Routledge,
      2004): 88.

16 Geoffrey Parker, *Europe in Crisis*, 1598–1648 (Ithaca: Cornell University Press, 1979): 15.

17 Marco Van Leeuwen et al, "Giving in the Golden Age: presentation of a new research project," *Paper for the Fourth Flemish-Dutch Conference of the economic and social history of the Low Countries before 1850* (January 2009): 4, http://www.lowcountries.nl/papers2009/papers2009_vanleeuwen.pdf.

18 Anne Elizabeth Conger McCants, *Civic Charity in a Golden Age* (Urbana: University of Illinois Press, 1997): 195.

19 Geoffrey Parker, *Europe in Crisis*, 1598–1648 (Ithaca: Cornell University Press, 1979): 16–17.

20 Edward H. Berman, *The Ideology of Philanthropy* (Albany: State University of New York Press, 1983): 1.

21 Natalia Dinello, "Elites and Philanthropy in Russia," *International Journal of Politics, Culture and Society*, Vol.12, No.1 (1998), II. Philanthropy in Russia and the United States: 120.

22 Ibid, 117.

23 Edward H. Berman, *The Ideology of Philanthropy* (Albany: State University of New York Press, 1983): 18.

24 Natalia Dinello, "Elites and Philanthropy in Russia," *International Journal of Politics, Culture and Society*, Vol.12, No.1 (1998), II. Philanthropy in Russia and the United States: 121.

25 Michael Tanner, *The End of Welfare: Fighting Poverty in Civil Society* (Cato Institute, 1996).

26 Edward H. Berman, *The Ideology of Philanthropy* (Albany: State University of New York Press, 1983).

27 *The Encyclopedia of Foreign Relations*, s.v. "The Cold War Foreign Aid Program, 1947–1953." http://www.americanforeignrelations.com/E-N/Foreign-Aid-The-cold-war-foreign-aid-program-1947-1953.html.

28 Ibid.

29 Ibid.

30 Pavol Fric, "Impact of 20th Century Fascism and Communism, Proletarian Altruism: The Case of the Czech Republic" (paper presented by the NGO School Foundation). http://www.ngoschool.ru/doc/ngo/05_Fric_Impact.pdf.

31 Natalia Dinello, "Elites and Philanthropy in Russia," *International Journal of Politics, Culture and Society*, Vol.12, No.1 (1998), II. Philanthropy in Russia and the United States: 117.

32 Ana Siljak, "Between East and West: Hegel and the Origins of the Russian Dilemma," *Journal of the History of Ideas*, Vol.62, No.2 (2001): 354.

33 Ibid.

34 Nicholas Churchich, *Marxism and Morality: A Critical Examination of Marxist Ethics* (Cambridge: James Clarke, 1994).

35 James Scanlan, "Nicholas Chernyshevsky and Philosophical Materialism in Russia," *Journal of the History of Philosophy*, Vol.8, No.1 (1970): 72.

36 Alexander Etkind, "Soviet Subjectivity: Torture for the Sake of Salvation?" *Kritika: Explorations in Russian and Eurasian History*, Vol.6, No.1 (2005): 176.

37 Ibid, 182.

38 Ibid, 175.

39 Kevin Kelly, *New Rules for the New Economy* (New York: Penguin Books, 1999). http://www.kk.org/newrules/contents.php.

40 Ibid.

41 Joanna Macy, "Spirituality and Security," *Whole Earth Catalog* (Copyright 2002 Point Foundation).

42 Eva Moskowitz, *In Therapy We Trust: America's Obsession with Self Fulfillment* (Baltimore: Johns Hopkins University Press, 2001): 230–233.

43 Howard Rheingold, *The Virtual Community: Homesteading on the Electronic Frontier* (Cambridge: MIT Press, 2000). http://www.rheingold.com.

44 *Whole Earth Catalogue*: http://www.wholeearth.com/about.php.Whole Earth 'Lectronic Link: http://www.well.com.

45 Howard Rheingold, *The Virtual Community: Homesteading on the Electronic Frontier* (Cambridge: MIT Press, 2000). http://www.rheingold.com.

Notes to Chapter 4: *Capacities*, pp 77–115

1 Janet I. Tu, "World Vision's Richard Stearns sets out to put an end to global poverty," *Seattle Times*, August 23, 2009.

2 Helmut Reisen, "The Multilateral Donor Non-System: Towards Accountability and Efficient Role Assignment," *OECD Development Center*, (2009): 3. http://www.economics-ejournal.org/economics/discussionpapers/2009-18.

3 "History of DAC lists of aid recipient countries," *Development Co-operation Directorate (DCD-DAC)*. http://www.oecd.org/document/55/0,3343,en_2649_34447_35832055_1_1_1_1,00.html.

4 Moisés Naím, "Rogue Aid," *Foreign Policy*, Vol. 159 (March/April 2007): 95.

5 Dr. Kevin J. Minch, "Bilateral vs Multilateral Aid," http://www.idebate.org/debatabase/topic_details.php?topicID=392.

6   James McGann and Mary Johnstone, "The Power Shift and the NGO Credibility Crisis," *The International Journal of Not-for-Profit Law*, Volume 8, 2, (Washington, DC: International Center for Not-for-Profit Law: 2006).

7   Bishwapriya Sanyal, Vinit Mukhija, "Institutional Pluralism and Housing Delivery: A Case of Unforeseen Conflicts in Mumbai, India", *World Development*, Vol. 29, No. 12, (Montreal: McGill University, 2001): 2054.

8   Enamul Habib, "The role of government and NGOs in slum development: the case of Dhaka City," *Development in Practice*, Vol. 19, No. 2, (2009): 260.

9   M. Shamsul Haque, "The Changing Balance of Power between the Government and NGOS in Bangladesh", *International Political Science Review*, Vol. 23, No. 4, (2002): 418–19.

10   Saleem Samad, "Political Squall Stalls Bangladesh Development Project" http://www.globalpolicy.org/component/content/article/176-general/32020.html

11   M. Shamsul Haque, "The Changing Balance of Power between the Government and NGOS in Bangladesh", *International Political Science Review*, Vol. 23, No. 4, (2002): 416.

12   Ibid. 421.

13   Ibid. 429.

14   Islam, Q. T., "Defining Pro-poor Intervention in Urban Health: The Case of Dhaka City," *CPD-UNFPA Publications* (2000).

15   Sheela Patel and Jockin Arputham, " An offer of partnership or a promise of conflict in Dharavi, Mumbai?," *Environment and Urbanization*, 19 (2007): 501.

16   James McGann and Mary Johnstone, "The Power Shift and the NGO Credibility Crisis," *International Journal of Not-for-Profit Law*, Vol. 8, No. 2 (2006).

17   Michael Yaziji and Jonathan Doh, "Part 1 Understanding NGOs", Excerpt *NGOs and Corporations: Conflict and Collaboration*, (Cambridge University Press, 2009).

18   Lester M. Salamon, "The Rise of the Nonprofit Sector,"*Foreign Affairs*, Vol. 73, No. 4 (1994): 114–5.

19   Stanley Fischer, Ernesto Hernández-Catá, and Mohsin S. Khan, "Africa: Is This the Turning Point? (International Monetary Fund Paper on Policy Analysis and Assessment, May 1998): 6.

20   Jessica T. Mathews, "Power Shift," *Foreign Affairs*, Vol. 76, No. 1 (1997): 51.

21   Lester M. Salamon, "The Rise of the Nonprofit Sector," *Foreign Affairs*, Vol. 73, No. 4 (1994): 114–5.

22   Ibid, 115.

23   Ibid, 114.

24   United Nations Framework Convention on Climate Change online documentation of The Kyoto Protocol Status of Ratification, as of July 8, 2009: http://unfccc.int/files/kyoto_protocol/status_of_ratification/application/pdf/kp_ratification_20090708.pdf.

25   Lester M. Salamon, "The Rise of the Nonprofit Sector," *Foreign Affairs*, Vol. 73, No. 4 (1994).

Notes to Chapter 5: *Challenges*, pp 117–147

1   Kenneth Anderson, "What NGO Accountability Means – and Does Not Mean," *American Journal of International Law*, Vol. 103, No. 1 (2009).

2   Jon Christensen, "Asking the Do-Gooders to Prove They Do Good," *New York Times*, January 3, 2004, Online Edition. http://www.nytimes.com/2004/01/03/arts/asking-the-do-gooders-to-prove-they-do-good.html?scp=1&sq=asking%20do-gooders%20to%20prove%20they%20do%20good&st=cse&pagewanted=1.

3   Andy Storey, "Non-Neutral Humanitarianism: NGOs and the Rwanda Crisis," *Development in Practice*, Vol. 7, No. 4 (1997): 384.

4   "Asian Bloc to Handle Burma Aid," thestar.com, May 19, 2008, Online, http://www.thestar.com/article/427381.

5   "In Myanmar, Loss, Grief and, for Some, Resignation," *New York Times*, May 27, 2008, Online Edition, http://www.nytimes.com/2008/05/27/world/asia/27scene.html?pagewanted=1&_r=1&sq=cyclone%20nargis&st=cse&scp=19_

6   Kenneth Denby, "Burma Cyclone: Up to 50,000 Dead and Millions Homeless, But Still No Call for Aid," *The Times*, May 7, 2008, Online Edition, http://www.timesonline.co.uk/tol/news/world/asia/article3883123.ece.

7   "DRT Americas Successfully Completes Mission to Pisco, Peru," *Deutsche Post DHL* website, http://www.dp-dhl.de/dp-dhl?skin=hi&check=no&lang=de_EN&xmlFile=2009853.

8   "Disaster Response," *Deutsche Post DHL* Video, Online, http://www.dp-dhl.de/dp-dhl?tab=1&skin=hi&check=no&lang=de_EN&xmlFile=2002216

9   Ibid.

10   Ibid.

11   R.E. Utley, *Major Powers and Peacekeeping: Perspectives, Priorities, and the Challenges of Military Intervention* (Aldershot: Ashgate Publishing, 2003): 3.

12   Jane Perlez, "U.N. Rwanda Rights Effort Is Hurt by Understaffing," *New York Times*, August 25, 1994, Online Edition, http://www.nytimes.com/1994/08/25/world/un-rwanda-rights-effort-is-hurt-by-understaffing.html.

13   Peter Utting, "Partnerships for Development or Privatization of the Multilateral System?" (Paper presented for the United Nations *Research Institute for Social Development* (UNRISD at a seminar organized by the North-South Coalition in Oslo, Norway, December 8, 2000), http://www.corpwatch.org/article.php?id=616.

14   Warren Sach, "UN Cash Position," (Report), May 9, 2008, http://www.un.org/ga/fifth/sach.un.cash.status.05.08.pdf.

15   "UNCTC Origins," *The United Nations Conference on Trade and Development* Website, http://unctc.unctad.org/aspx/UNCTCOrigins.aspx.

16   Jane Nelson, *The United Nations and the Private Sector: A Framework for Collaboration* (New York: Global Compact Office, United Nations, 2008). http://www.unglobalcompact.org/docs/news_events/9.1_news_archives/2008_09_24/UN_Business_Framework.pdf

17   "Disaster Response," *Deutsche Post DHL* Video, Online, http://www.dp-dhl.de/dp-d hl?tab=1&skin=hi&check=no&lang=d e_EN&xmlFile=2002216

18   "In Wake of Criticism, Nature Conservancy Changes Policies," *New York Times*, June 14, 2003, Online Edition. http://www.nytimes.com/2003/06/14/national/14CND-NATU.html?pagewanted=print&.

19   Laurie Garret, "The Challenge of Global Health," *Foreign Affairs*, Vol. 86, No. 1 (2007).

20   Andy Storey, "Non-Neutral Humanitarianism: NGOs and the Rwanda Crisis," *Development in Practice*, Vol. 7, No. 4 (1997): 384–394.

21   William Easterly, *The White Man's Burden: Why the West's Efforts to Aid the Rest Have Done So Much Ill and So Little Good* (New York: Penguin 2006): 154.

22   Angelo Bonfiglioli, "Empowering the Poor: Local Governance for Poverty Reduction" (paper presented by the *United Nations Capital Development Fund* in November 2003), Online. http://unpan1.un.org/intradoc/groups/public/documents/un/unpan010168.pdf.

23   Sonia Shah, "Why Africa Doesn't Want Aid," *The Nation*, March 17, 2009, Foreign Affairs Section, Online Edition. http://www.thenation.com/doc/20090330/shah.

24   "Untying Aid to the LDCs," *OECD Observer* (2001), Online http://www.oecd.org/dataoecd/16/24/2002959.pdf.

25   "Inefficiency, Costs Gobble Up US Emergency Food Aid," *Environment News Service* (2007), Online Edition. http://www.ens-newswire.com/ens/apr2007/2007-04-19-05.asp.

26   Peter Nunnenkamp, "The Myth of NGO Superiority," *Global Policy Forum*. http://www.globalpolicy.org/component/content/article/176/31437.html.

27   "The World Bank and Development Assistance," Testimony Prepared by Joseph E. Stigliz, For presentation before the House Financial Services Committee," May 22, 2007, Online. http://www.house.gov/financialservices/hearing110/htstiglitz052207.pdf.

28   Demba Moussa Dembélé, "Aid dependence and the MDGs," *Pambazuka News*, September 08, 2005, Online. http://www.pambazuka.org/en/category/features/29376.

29   Dambisa Moyo, *Dead Aid: Why Aid is not working and how there is a better way for Africa* (New York: Farrar, Straus and Giroux, 2009).

30   Chantal Dupasquier and Patrick N. Osakwe, "Foreign Direct Investment in Africa: Performance, Challenges and Responsibilities" (Work in Progress No. 21 presented by the *African Trade Policy Centre*, September 2005), Online. http://www.uneca.org/atpc/Work%20in%20progress/21.pdf.

31   Will Connors, "Oil Firms Slam Nigeria's Bid to Overhaul Energy Industry," *The Wall Street Journal*, July 29, 2009, Business Section, Online Edition. http://online.wsj.com/article/SB124881906475587991.html.

Notes to Chapter 6: *Exchange*, pp 149–205

1   Pierre Bourdieu, *Outline of a Theory of Practice* (Cambridge: Cambridge University Press, 1977).

2   Ibid.

3   W. L. Wheaton, T. J. Kent, Jr. and M. M. Webber, "Catherine Bauer Wurster, City and Regional Planning: Berkeley," University of California: In Memoriam, April 1966. University of California Calisphere (2007). http://content.cdlib.org/view?docId=hb658 006rx&brand=calisphere; M. Ijlal Muzaffar, "The Periphery Within: Modern Architecture and the Making of the Third Word" (PhD diss., Massachusetts Institute of Technology, 2007): 25.

4   Jacob L. Crane, "The World-Wide Housing Problem," *Town Planning Review*, Vol. 22 (1951): 1–16. http://www.fao.org/DOCREP/X5350E/x5350e04.htm; M. Ijlal Muzaffar, "The Periphery Within: Modern Architecture and the Making of the Third Word" (PhD diss., Massachusetts Institute of Technology, 2007): 43–81.

5   Nathalie de Mazieres, "Homage," *Environmental Design, Journal of the Islamic Environmental Design Research Centre*, Vol. 1 (1985): 22–25; M. Ijlal Muzaffar, "The Periphery Within: Modern Architecture and the Making of the Third Word" (PhD diss., Massachusetts Institute of Technology, 2007):101–285.

6   http://www.habitat.org/how/factsheet.aspx

7   http://www.habitat.org/how/carter.aspx

8   http://www.habitat.org/how/millard.aspx

9   For this discussion in full, see Chris Anderson, *Free: The Future of Radical Price*, (New York: Hyperion 2007) and Malcom Gladwell, "Price to Sell," *New Yorker Magazine*, July 6, 2009.

10   Ed Hale, telephone interview, July 17, 2009.

11   http://www.habitat.org/gv/factsheet_international.aspx

12   Leslie Eaton and Stephanie Strom, "Volunteer Group Lags in Replacing Gulf Homes," *New York Times*, February 22, 2007, Online Edition, http://www.nytimes.com/2007/02/22/us/22habitat.html?pagewanted=1&_r=1.

13   Javier Viera, telephone interview, July 22, 2009.

14   Gina Buffone, telephone interview, July 20, 2009.

15   Javier Viera, telephone interview, July 22, 2009.

16   http://www.habitat.org/housing_finance/partnerships.aspx

17   Gus Burns, "Saginaw Fights Blight: The Upside of Urban Decay," *The Saginaw News*, Friday, August 14, 2009.

18   V. Baweja, "A Pre-history of Green Architecture: Otto Koenigsberger and Tropical Architecture, from Pincely Mysore to Post-colonial London" (PhD diss., The University of Michigan, 2008), 7–10, 19–22, 28–31; Rhodri Windsor Liscombe, "Independence: Otto Koenigsberger and Modernist Urban Resettlement in India," *Planning Perspectives*, Vol. 21 (2006): 157–178. M. Ijlal Muzaffar, "The Periphery Within: Modern Architecture and the Making of the Third Word" (PhD diss., Massachusetts Institute of Technology, 2007):101–267

19   Richard Harris, "The Silence of the Experts: 'Aided Self-help Housing', 1939–1954," *Habitat International*, Vol. 22, No. 2 (1998): 165–189; Bernard Taper, "Charles Abrams in Ghana," *Habitat International*, Vol. 5 (1980): 49–53. selected passage from *The New Yorker*, Vol. 43, February 11, 1967; M. Ijlal Muzaffar, "The Periphery Within: Modern Architecture and the Making of the Third Word" (PhD diss., Massachusetts Institute of Technology, 2007): 33–78, 101–267

20   C.A. Doxiadis, *Ekistics: An introduction to the Science of Human Settlements* (Oxford University Press, London, 1968).

21   Panayiota I. Pyla, "Hassan Fathy Revisited: Postwar Discourses on Science, Development, and Vernacular Architecture," *Journal of Architectural Education*, Vol. 60 (2007): 28–39.

22   Ana Laura Ruesjas, "The Mexicali Experimental Project: An Analysis of Its Changes" (MA diss., McGill University, 1997), 23–68.

23   Koos Bosma, Dorine van Hoogstraten, Martijn Vos eds., *Housing For the Millions, John Habraken and the SAR* (1960–2000) (Rotterdam: NAI, 2000), 20–70. http://www.habraken.com.

24   T.C. Wong et al., ed. Spatial Planning for a Sustainable Singapore (Springer, 2008), 183–204; Liu Thai Ker, "Improving the Living Environment of Singapore," *Environmental Monitoring and Assessment*, Vol. 19 (1991): 251–259.

25   Hasan-Uddin Khan, ed. *Charles Correa: Architect in India* (London: Butterworth Architecture, 1987): 44–80; Charles Correa, "An Essay for JAE," *Journal of Architectural Education*, Vol. 40 (1987): 12.

26   Ray Bromley, "Peru 1957–1977: How Time and Place Influenced John Turner's Ideas on Housing Policy," *Habitat International*, Vol. 27 (2003): 271–929; Herbert Werlin, "The Slum Upgrading Myth," *Urban Studies*, Vol. 36, No. 9 (1999): 1523–1533.

27   Enrique Penalosa, "Parks for Livable Cities: Lessons from a Radical Mayor," *Places*, Vol. 15, No. 3 (2003): 30–33.

28   "Cameron Sinclair ICON 047", *Iconeye*, May 2007, Online, http://www.iconeye.com, http://www.architectureforhumanity.org/.

29   Mark Jacobson, "Mumbai's Shadow City," *National Geographic Magazine*, Online Edition, http://ngm.nationalgeographic.com/2007/05/dharavi-mumbai-slum/jacobson-text.html; "Building New 'Ecosystems' in Mumbai's Slums: India Knowledge@Wharton," University of Pennsylvania, Online. http://knowledge.wharton.upenn.edu/india/article.cfm?articleid=4223.

1   Krishna Mazumdar, "An Analysis of Causal
    Flow Between Social Development and
    Economic Growth: The Social Development
    Index," *American Journal of Economics and
    Sociology*, Vol. 55, No. 3 (1996): 362.
2   Ibid.
3   Harris and Buzzelli, "House Building in the
    Machine Age, 1920s–170s: Realities and
    Perceptions of Modernization in North
    America and Australia," *Business History*,
    Vol. 47, No. 1, (2005): 59–85.
4   R. Harris and C. Giles, "A mixed message: the
    agents and forms of international housing
    policy, 1945–1973," *Habitat International*, Vol.
    27 (2003): 176.
5   USAID Policy Paper, Urban Development
    Policy, Bureau for Program and Policy
    Coordination, *U.S. Agency for International
    Development*, (Washington, D.C., October
    1984).
6   Critical Literature Review of the Human
    Development Indices, UNDP, Prepared for
    the UNDP Practicum in International Affairs,
    (2009), Powerpoint, Online. http://www.gpia.
    info/files/practicum/28/UNDP%20HDR.ppt.
7   Ibid.
8   http://econlog.econlib.org/
    archives/2009/05/against_the_hum.html.
9   Foreign Direct Investment for Development,
    "Maximising Benefits, Minimising Costs,"
    OECD Report, (2002).

Image Credits

8

Index

DEMINING

Blaster, ohmmeter
Digital meter that registers the value
of circuit resistance.

Bomb locator, Ferex Forester
Detects and maps ammunition, explosives or chemical pollutants with
ferromagnetic constituents.

Detector, metal, MTD 7
A hand-held mine detector suitable for
all theaters of operation.

Exploder, blasting machine, CD-450
Offers a range of power and voltage
in a compact, portable, and durable
enclosure.

Locator, magnetic
Hand-held metallic mine detector.

DRUGS AND MEDICAL EQUIPMENT

Abortion, management of complications
Helps to treat complications of abortion and miscarriage, including sepsis
and incomplete evacuation.

Burn dressing module
Designed for nursing staff; contains forty dressings (the average equivalent of eight days in a post-op ward).

Clinical delivery assistance kit
Midwifery kit equipped to meet the needs of normal deliveries but also to assist in emergency situations.

Emergency health kit, without malaria module
Designed to supply health center units treating common diseases with enough drugs, medical equipment, and renewable supplies for ten patients over three months.

Emergency kit, diarrhea diseases, Italian
Supplies for treating 100 severe and 400 moderate cases of cholera, and 200 cases of Shigella dysentery.

Emergency kit, diarrhea profile, Italian

Drugs to prevent and control 100 cases of diarrheal diseases.

Emergency kit, support to diarrhea, Italian

Medical supplies to prevent and control 100 cases of diarrheal diseases, to be used with diarrhea profile.

Emergency kit, support to trauma, Italian

Medical supplies enough to treat 100 trauma cases.

Emergency kit, trauma profile, Italian

Drugs to treat 100 trauma cases, to be used with trauma kit.

First aid kit, ten persons

Intended as first-line treatment for common ailments and minor injuries, to be used by personnel in areas with inadequate healthcare facilities.

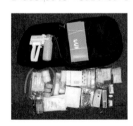

First aid kit, individual

Intended as first-line treatment for common ailments and minor injuries, to be used by personnel in areas with inadequate healthcare facilities.

First aid kit, office

Intended as first-line treatment for common ailments and minor injuries, to be used by personnel in areas with inadequate healthcare facilities.

Medical, individual-travel kit

This kit is designed for use by personnel deployed in areas where healthcare facilities are inadequate or unavailable, to be used as first-line treatment of common ailments and minor injuries.

Trauma kit, large

Designed for use in the pre-hospital resuscitation phase of major trauma; contains fifty selected items of medicine and equipment required to assess, treat and stabilize injured person(s) immediately.

Trauma kit, mini

A scaled-down Trauma kit of all three modules supplied in a waterproof carry bag and intended for small teams, as it has been set-up for sub-office use.

ELECTRICITY DEVICES

Electrical kit for room, prefabricated

Used to link accommodation units to power sources such as generators.

Generator, diesel, 5kva, with lamp
Ideal for emergency lighting or long-term power to living/office accommodation units.

F.G. Wilson Generator, diesel, 27 kva, wheel-mounted
One of a family of industrial generators used for lighting and pumping water at hospitals, large camps and compounds.

Generator, diesel, 3.5 kva, Kubota
Compact, lightweight generator rugged enough for heavy duty work, yet portable enough for dispersed deployment.

Parts, trailer and sound-attenuated
Used for power in hospitals, camps, secured areas and is sound attenuated.

234

Generator, diesel, 14 kva,
wheel-mounted
Provides power in emergency situations
and is easily adaptable

Generator, diesel, 15 kva,
wheel-mounted
A light set that provides electrical
power in emergency situations and is
easily adaptable to any use, such as
in hospitals, camps and for exterior
lighting in secured areas.

Generator, diesel, 17.5, wheel-mounted
Designed to provide continuous electrical power (at variable load) when
commercially purchased power is not
available.

Generator, diesel, 20 kva,
wheel-mounted
Used to provide electrical power in
any emergency.

Generator, diesel engine, 420 Vatt-14V
Compact, lightweight generators rugged
enough for heavy use but easily
deployable.

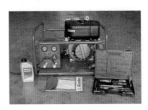

Generator, petrol engine, 12.5 kva, 110 V
Provides power in emergency hospitals and camps.

Lamp, solar
Designed for regions without electricity; also supplies DC power.

Lighting equipment, telescopic, wheel-mounted
A mobile, compact and versatile floodlight trailer.

Meter, light
Good for monitoring light levels in lux or foot Candles.

Voltage stabilizer, automatic

Used for high power applications requiring a sinusoidal load voltage independent of line voltage variations for laboratories, radio equipment, air conditioning equipment, household appliances, and machines.

FOOD ITEMS

Compact food, BP-5

A complete, fully-balanced food concentrate for maintaining or restoring normal physical health; contains only four percent moisture, and can be consumed dry or with water.

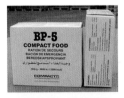

High energy biscuits, 6 kg

Emergency sustenance; may be used in therapeutic feeding programs or immediate response.

High energy biscuits, 10 kg

Emergency sustenance; may be used in therapeutic feeding programs or immediate response.

Ration meal, ready to eat, vegetarian

To be eaten anywhere, anytime; these rations are packaged in a triple-layer foil/plastic "retort" pouch to extend storage-life.

INDIVIDUAL KIT AND SAFETY ITEMS

Helmet, ballistic
Protect the user's head against impact and ballistic hazards.

Vest, ballistic
Provides protection from bullets, fragmenting munitions and debris from explosives.

Blanket, ballistic, Chevrolet K20
Used to protect vehicle occupants, though its effectiveness isn't fully known by the manufacturer.

Blanket, ballistic, Toyota Land Cruiser LHD
A precaution taken to increase the safety of field staff.

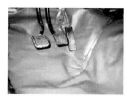

Detector, intruder, cordless
Uses passive infrared technology to announce when there are intruders.

Detector, smoke

Photoelectric smoke detector and fire alarm recommended for installation in all occupied rooms.

Fire extinguisher, 6 kg

Suitable for all types of fire, this refillable extinguisher is approved in accordance with BS EN ISO9002.

Fire extinguisher, 50 kg

Dry chemical powder can effectively control ordinary combusting materials and fires under electric tension.

Fridge, car

Energy-efficient electric cooler keeps food and drink at temperature without using CFCs.

Fridge / freezer, field

An energy-efficient electric cooler made of insulating foam to keep food and drink at temperature.

Individual kit, "Rapid Response Team"

Meets the basic needs of one person when deployed to remote areas, including food and cooking supplies, hygiene and sanitation items, shelter supplies and water treatment equipment.

OFFICE AND LIVING ACCOMMODATIONS

Ablution unit, prefab., hard wall
Easy-install ablution structure
equipped with a shower, mirror,
toilet, washbasin, fans, boiler and
electrical.

Living, accommodation unit, 2 people,
ancillaries, part 2
A single unit fit to accommodate
two persons.

Office, accommodation unit, two people,
ancillaries, part 2
A single unit fit to accommodate
two persons.

Prefabricated, ablution unit,
hard wall
Easy-install ablution structure
equipped with a shower, mirror,
toilet, washbasin, fans, boiler
and electrical.

Prefabricated, conference room, hard wall

Six standard prefabricated rooms joined side by side, pre-wired with lights, power points, data/communication box and HVAC.

Prefabricated, living, hard wall, with accessories

Living accommodation unit for two pre-wired with lights, power points, HVAC and is fully furnished.

Prefabricated, office, hard wall, with accessories

Office for two, fully furnished and pre-wired with lights, power points, data/communication box and HVAC.

Prefabricated, operation room, hard wall

Six standard prefabricated rooms joined side by side, pre-wired with lights, power points, data/communication box and HVAC.

Roof, secondary, standard room prefabricated

A kit contains two secondary roofs, three rafters and six connection profiles

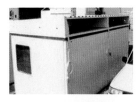

Toilet, field with accessories
Portable environmental toilet with
waste bag kits and a privacy tent
inside the backpack.

RADIO AND TELECOMMUNICATION

Megaphone, handled
Audible enough for small groups of
twenty to thirty people.

SANITATION AND HYGIENE

Bags, body
Bags used to transport corpses.

Digging tools
Used to prepare sites for
construction.

Mosquito net
Protects the body from mosquitoes
bites.

Pickaxe with handle
Used to prepare sites for construction.

Soap bar
Multipurpose soap for bathing and laundry.

Spade with varnished ash and grip
Used to prepare sites for construction.

Stretcher, fixed handles with securing straps
Transports injured persons; good over difficult terrain.

Squatting plate, latrines
Sanitation device situated over a trench.

Thermal evacuation bag
Insulates body from hypothermia and reduces effects of shock.

Thermal hood, universal
Insulates head from extreme heat loss.

Blanket, quilted
Designed for cold climates and made
from recycled textiles.

Bag, polypropylene woven, empty
Good for transporting dry foodstuffs.

Blanket, UNHCR, 30% wool
Intended for refugee camps and
emergency situations.

Blanket, 50% wool 50% new fibers
Combined content provides relief in
coldest climates, also flame retardant.

Blanket 50% wool 50% synthetic fibers
Intended to be provided to victims of
natural or man-made disasters.

Cooking set
Equipped to prepare meals for a family
of five.

Kitchen set, family type
Equipped to prepare meals for a family of five.

Overshoes, men
Waterproof shoe coverings.

Plastic rolls, 4 × 60 mt
Used to fashion temporary shelters.

Tarpaulin, woven plastic, 4 × 6 mt
Heavy-duty textile used for temporary shelters.

Tarpaulins, woven plastic, 4 × 60 mt
Heavy-duty textile used for temporary shelters.

Tent, for cold climate, 22 sq.m.
Ferrino
Multipurpose single tent.

Tent, for cold climate, 24 sq.m., Gammax
Utilized as dwelling for multiple people.

Tent, for warm climate, 24 sq.m. Gammax
Built for cold, rough climates with an efficient insulation system and stable configuration.

Tent, multipurpose, 32 sq.m. approx
This type of tent has been developed for recovering in cold areas; used as office accommodation, mess-room, field hospital and dressing station.

5,10 m

5,82 m

Tent, multipurpose, 38-42 sq.m.
Can be used as a single dwelling or complete camp.

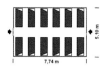

5,10 m

7,74 m

Tent P.I 88
Versatile tent; often used as a sanitation facility.

TOOLS

Cramps
Fasteners for wire fencing.

Rope, polypropylene, 8mm twisted
Only rope which floats.

Tool kit
Standard tools for general use.

Tool kit with step ladders for
ablution unit
Standard tools for general use.

Tool kit with step ladders for room
prefabricated
Standard tools for general use.

Toyota Hi Lux Pick up, Double cab,
3.0 diesel, 4 × 4 DC, RHD
Effective as both a passenger car and
material transport vehicle.

Boat, inflatable, with engine,
accessories & safety jack
Used for disaster rescue operations,
especially during flooding.

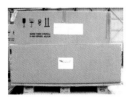

Jerry can, collapsible, with screw
cap, 10 liters
Collapsible bags to transport, store
and distribute water.

Jerry can, collapsible, with zip,
10 liters
Collapsible bags to transport, store
and distribute water.

Jerry cans for water, plastic,
5 gallons
Collapsible bags to transport, store
and distribute water.

Water distribution ramp, 6 hi-flow taps

Ramps used for the distribution of water. It can be used either for water storage containers or truck water tanks.

Water drinking emergency kit, filter

Small filters for families, lasting approx. 6–12 months.

Water purification unit, 4 cu.m/hrs

Delivers potable water using available surface water.

Water purification unit, 4 cu.m/hrs, Emwat

Equipped to store and distribute water for up to 20,000 people.

Water purification unit.
15 cu.m/hrs, Aquasen
Compact, portable treatment plant.

Water pump, diesel, 2'' x 2'',
wheel mounted
Lifts deep groundwater in arid regions
and pressurizes water through a
pipeline.

Water storage container, 1000 lt,
collapsible, 2 x 2 mt
Portable container made of PVC-
coated polyester fabric for UV-intense
regions.

Water tank, collapsible, 1,000 lt,
with harness
Transport tanks that fit a standard
truck bed.

Water tank, collapsible, 1,000 lt,
with ramp
Limited-capacity tanks (stores one
day's supply of water).

Water tank, collapsible, 3,500 lt,
with 2 distribution ramp and harness
Used to distribute water during
disasters.

Water tank, collapsible, 5,000 lt,
with harness
Plated tanks mountable to a truck.

Water tank, collapsible, 7,500 lt,
with 2 distribution ramp and harness
Used to distribute water during
disasters.

Water tank, collapsible, 10,000 lt,
with 2 distribution ramps
Used to distribute water during
disasters.

WAREHOUSING AND HANDLING EQUIPMENT

Box, storage and transit
Trunk for storing and delivering
clothing, electrical and other
valuables.

Forklift truck, diesel Model DP40K
Optimal for outdoor use.

Forklift truck, electric, 2.5 mt
Optimal for warehouse use.

Pallet, plastic, 1.2 × 1 × 1.45 mt
Used to package, transport and
insulate perishable items.

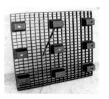

Prefabricated, warehouse,
soft wall, 7 × 9 mt
A compact enclosure for ten, suitable
for office and living accommodations.

Prefabricated, warehouse, soft wall,
10 x 24 m
Warehousing for emergency goods,
hospital facilities and temporary
housing.

Prefabricated, warehouse, soft wall,
10 x 24 m, ALU structure
Similar structure, but built using
aluminum members instead of steel for
safety and ease of handling.

Prefabricated, warehouse, soft wall,
10 x 32 m, ALU structure
Also built using aluminum members
instead of steel for safety and ease
of handling.

Prefabricate, warehouse, softwall,
THPA
Tent-like structure optimized for
rapid deployment and relocation and
used for field operations and housing.

Prefabricated, warehouse, THAB
10 x 24 m
Built using pinned-together framing
and rigid bracing to withstand very
high loads.

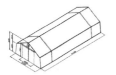

Scale, warehouse, 200 kg
Used for measuring foodstuffs.